THE INDIGO HOURS

Writers Walk the Night

–

Introduced and edited by

Duncan Minshull

Notting Hill Editions

Published in 2026
by Notting Hill Editions Ltd
Mirefoot, Burneside, Kendal, LA8 9AB

EU authorised representative
Easy Access System Europe
Mustamäe tee 50, 10621 Tallinn, Estonia
easproject.com
gpsr.reequests@easproject.com

Series design by FLOK Design, Berlin, Germany
Cover design by Matthew Burne

Typeset by CB Editions, London
Printed and bound by Imago Group

A CIP record for this book is available from the British Library

ISBN 978-1-912559-77-0

nottinghilleditions.com

'There is something otherworldly about night-walking. Something that makes you see the world differently.'

– Shane O'Mara

'It grows dark. Life jingles, toots, and hammers.'

– Joseph Roth

Contents

– Introduction –

xiii

– W. G. SEBALD –

The Curtain Rises

1

– EDITH WHARTON –

The Stage is Set

2

– VERNON LEE –

With Moving Blobs

6

– EDWARD LEAR –

Between Civility and Morpheus

9

– LESLIE STEPHEN –

The Wrong Way at 7.30 p.m.

11

– HERMAN MELVILLE –

Lanterns, Assassins, Impressions

17

– HENRY DAVID THOREAU–

The Dark is Medicinal

19

Different Shades of Dark

22

– MARY MORRIS –

It's Only Nine O'clock

24

– CAROL LAKE –

The Moon Shines Bright on Charlie Chaplin

27

– CHRISTIANE RITTER –

The Extinction of All Colours

28

– JOHANN PAUL FRIEDRICH RICHTER –

Starlight Parties

31

– DOROTHY WORDSWORTH –

Hootings

32

– RICHARD JEFFERIES –

'Ching Ching' and 'Twit Twit'

34

– JOHN MUIR –

All Manner of Sounds

35

– GEORGE ORWELL –
The Stars are a Free Show
36

More Stars
38

– JOANNA KAVENNA –
We Are Made of Stardust
41

– NICHOLAS SHAKESPEARE –
Sancho Takes on a Spectral Glimmer
43

– D. H. LAWRENCE –
Black, Black, Black
45

– LOREN EISELEY –
Towards the Streetlights
49

– ROBERT LOUIS STEVENSON –
Lighting the City
51

More Lights
56

– THÉOPHILE GAUTIER –
Suspicious Lights
58

– JEAN-PAUL CLÉBERT –
With Ectoplasmic Ease
61

– THOMAS DE QUINCEY –
Saturday Nights
62

– JOHN BURROUGHS –
Sunday Night
64

– RAINER MARIA RILKE –
Midnight Mass?
65

– CHARLES DICKENS –
At Half-Past Twelve
67

– LEIGH HUNT –
At One
71

– LOGAN PEARSALL SMITH –
The Word
78

– KATE PULLINGER –
Walk Number One, or Walk Number Two?
80

– THOMAS CORYAT –
Braves
85

– JACK LONDON –
Road Kids and Stiffs, and Bindle-Stiffs
86

– JOHN BROWN –
I Travelled by Night, that Being the Safe Time
89

– FANNY KEMBLE –
My Father Proposed a Walk
93

– ETHEL LYNN –
Night Cap
97

– ANNABEL ABBS –
Discombobulated Journey
98

– TIFFANY FRANCIS BAKER –
Remember To . . .
101

– VIRGINIA WOOLF –
In the Darkness the Brain Constructs a Scheme of the World
102

– FRANZ KAFKA –
The Second
105

– HILAIRE BELLOC –
A Third
106

– VICTOR HUGO –
Los Demonios? Contrabandistas?
107

– JOSEPH ADDISON –
Night Heightens the Awfulness of the Place
111

– MARY KINGSLEY –
Witches Eating Crabs
114

– RACHEL CARSON –
Ghost Crab
116

– AMELIA B. EDWARDS –
Gleaming Teeth
117

– JOHN HILLABY –
Headless
120

– LIEUTENANT CHARLES I. HALT –
Unexplained at Approximately 0300
123

– W. H. HUDSON –
A Little Before 3.45 a.m.
124

– EDWARD THOMAS –
The Night Had Gone
128

– FLORENCE FENWICK MILLER –
Before Daylight
131

More Dawns
133

– Acknowledgements –
135

DUNCAN MINSHULL

– Introduction –

As the light fades and darkness falls . . . let's bid a good evening to the walker-readers out there. To you, especially, who is about to follow a variety of feet across the pages of *The Indigo Hours*, and hear how the owners of such feet – be they large or small, bare or booted, lone or grouped – face the same striking truth on their journeys. And how the truth has to do with transformation.

The journeys to come are caught in journals, letters and diaries, ranging from the 1600s to the present day. They record feet that move along the streets of great cities and along the tracks of tame and unruly nature, in all its settings. Feet that move through the dying embers of evening, through the moonlight, through the artificial lights (called the 'urban stars'), and on towards the break of dawn. And feet that move through an array of blues and near blues, as the night is imbued with 'cobalt' and 'azure', 'cerulean' and 'mauve', 'indigo' and . . . well, perhaps you can find some others.

The blues tell half the story. Transformation of everything tells the whole, as these hundred or so feet make their ways across the world. But I'll defer to one of the walker-writers now, open to the changes, and observing that:

> Few walk by night. It is a very different season. On all sides novelties present themselves. Who would have believed it? The smallest recesses in the rocks are dim and cavernous . . . a distant cliff looks like a phosphorescent space on a hillside . . .

And as his (booted) feet keep moving:

> . . . every plant and field and forest emits its odour now . . . we hear the tinkling of rills which we never detected before . . . the rocks retain all night the warmth of the sun which they have absorbed. And so does the sand – if you dig a few inches into it you will find a warm bed.

So, sweet dreams to Henry David Thoreau in his bed of sand; who speaks for most of us, doesn't he? It's why he roams ahead. Believing that what he sees at night is unknown to him (as edges turn hazy and colours leech out); that the sounds and the smells of the countryside over-rule the sights; that these other senses attain a sharpness to the point of oddity, surreality. Be ready for this to happen. Things are not what they seem. And, as he will tell us, almost amusedly, 'Who would have believed it?'

Thoreau set off near Concord, Massachusetts, solo and unlighted, in the 1840s. But his sensory experiences speak for any age. For Nicholas Shakespeare in a Wiltshire lane, almost hit by a delivery van, its wheels dangerously hushed here. Yet, he explains, a lion is primed to roar at dawn to launch *its* sounds across the damp air. Big cats aren't heard on Kate Pullinger's urban outing; often there is little to note except a love of street lighting, a 'sparkle' of neon and florescence and sodium, that draws attention to a woman walking. A woman having to be alert and, aside from Pullinger, a number of others note the same.

Pullinger bestows the word sparkle on artificial lights, which usually diminish nature's own lights – the stars. Ah, the stars! It was fun to fill *The Indigo Hours* with as many as I could catch, falling or otherwise. Their sparkle is infinite; they are named after gods and mythical figures (Aldebaran and Orion, Sirius and Pleiades gaze down on human counterparts), and they surrender such compelling stories. Also, they help us when we need them most, keep us company and show us the way. The North Star, for one, has always been a friend to the trepidatious night walker.

*

As the light fades and darkness falls . . . so does human behaviour transform. You'll meet an unlikely duo of W.G. Sebald and Edith Wharton early in the collection. Unlikely, yes, but they share one thing during their dusky strolls – their views of a world turning performative. Daylight vistas begin to resemble stage-sets under lamplight. For Wharton it is the passers-by who respond in kind, becoming self-conscious and ceremonial as the hours darken. They act out characters close to the 'generic', as in a comedy by Carlo Goldoni, and even a pet dog, a Pomeranian, has a strut-on part to play. Wharton is casting her satiric eye over a square in lively provincial Italy. But what is it about these effects of the night, wherever it happens to be?

The occasions are numerous and varied. See how the night turns genial watchmen into 'animals' in 1820s London; how the Edwardian middle-classes turn into 'squabblers' at Mont-Saint-Michel; and on the boulevards of 1950s Paris witness the passing of 'an alarming number of dingbats' – nervy nocturnalists, who pause to peer at cats and children playing, after the moon climbs higher in the sky.

Under the moon children are always heading off. Small feet are heard to patter. Though the more I rounded them up, the more I found them to be indifferent to the delights of the night. Kate Pullinger, again, is busy 'herding' five-year-olds through town; she is open to everything, while her charges are too absorbed in each other to see and sense as much – it's understandable. Pitiless are Jack London's hobo 'road-kids', patrolling their patches, marking their prey, convinced that this is what the dark is really for. Then, Zarina and friends march mile upon mile and couldn't care less about a definite outcome. But at least Carol Lake's larky girls salute the phenomenon that helps their journey back:

> 'The moon shines bright on Charlie Chaplin,
> His boots are cracking, his boots are cracking . . .

We sing our way home; the moon rises up at the end of the street, shining straight into our path.'

*

The animals and squabblers, the dingbats and road kids – they enjoy a certain release and glee en route. But the changes at night also bring on a 'Fearness' – a fear, felt personally, by the walker-writers themselves, not just their subjects mentioned. The trouble is, many writers are beguiled by the stories that exist, are prey to what's been said and scripted down the years.

Out there you'll encounter Joseph Addison on his Walk of Aged Elms. Who thinks the dark won't unsettle him with its unknowable 'noises'. Who thinks the rumour of the Shape Of The Black Horse Without An Head unsettles merely those of 'weak mind'. Oh to believe such guff! And yet . . . the further this finely-tuned rationalist steps amongst the trees, in deepest Worcestershire, the more unsettled *he* will grow. Step by step, thought by thought, fancy by fancy, the link is made between forward motion and mounting dread. A second headless tale (about The Headless Indian) will spook the walk of John Hillaby. And a tale about the witches of the Gold Coast, 'emitting bright lights', will do the same for Mary Kingsley.

If these and other stories fail to stop the writers in their tracks – for stories can be ignored, even discounted – then experience itself might do the trick. In other words, facing a 'Fearness' that is real and not scripted. Seasoned hikers will fear failure on a French peak ('we were afraid to take the wrong way'), as others will fear oblivion in an Italian valley ('the solitude of night seemed to fill the horizon'); and inevitably there is everybody's fear: of chancing upon someone, or something, en route. What to do if 'each of us became aware of the presence of a *third . . .*'

In darkness 'dense' (too dense to see the lovely blues) another figure has just departed, hastily. Once again, amplified and awful noises will carry across the cooling air (*what* did I hear?), and confusion reigns, as if this man is stuck on a looping track to nowhere when he should be going somewhere. His plans turn to hunches, his doubts turn to 'terror'. Still, now is the right time to walk for an escapee, for a 'runaway' called John Brown. It's an oft-tramped way for many like him; from the rice and cotton fields of the south to the conurbations of the north, eventually guided by the sparkle of the North Star and aiming for the 'urban stars' of Chicago or Kansas City. Terror is endured, he says, because denseness offers cover on such journeys. Journeys taking weeks, that are not recreational or meditative or creative, but born of basic survival.

*

You went out at night . . . *walking?* Edith Wharton and Vernon Lee set forth, taking it easy, sauntering the hours and places well lit – the paseo and passeggiata hours of pleasing Mediterranean places – and are accompanied by friends or chaperoned by locals. Fanny Kemble and Amelia B. Edwards enjoy similar excursions. But, isn't it because their experiences *are* easy and organised, that hardly anything in their writing relates directly to a woman walking at night? Why, and how, do they go? It is left to others to consider this proposition – the woman who ventures alone, down an uncertain road, with bolder aims.

The GR4, part of the renowned Grande Randonnée network in southern France, is walked by one to ward off grief. At sunset, rather lost, the trail takes on a different hue and feel; more so after resting in a ruin and reading from a book entitled *Pourquoi la nuit est-elle noire?* – which says the night sky is proof of a finite universe, that humans are made of 'stardust', that after death we never wholly disappear. It's food for thought, and also sleep-inducing.

But later, what will tug at Joanna Kavenna's foot to wake her up? A pale lunatic, a moon spirit, or might it be the ghost of a late father? Assume something unnatural in this natural setting – and be surprised.

Annabel Abbs has bolder aims too, on a trip to New Mexico. But in Santa Fe she describes the sort of trouble that would keep a lot of us indoors. Unending is the emptiness of its suburbs, its poor and crumbled pavements, exposing the walker to bouts of crazy truck-driving. Then, out front, a solitary figure approaches – who will unsettle who first! A McDonald's neon offers Abbs some relief, before a desire is felt to roam anywhere in the world except these shadowy quarters of an Amercian city; a desire for the light and peopled places enjoyed by Wharton et al. A desire for the playgrounds of Europe, really.

Walking can lead to moments of composition; think of all the poets who build up their lines and their meters from the rhythms of their journeys. Follow Mary Morris down a dirt track in rural Mexico – no lights, no homeward pavements – and you get the sense she has composed a note-to-self to bolster her future footsteps. She knows the odds are against her, how it's been for others too, and how to respond to the hard miles: 'It is not easy to move in the world alone, and it is never easy for a woman. You must keep your wits about you.'

And she makes provision for her own bold walking: 'You mustn't get into dark places you can't get out of. Keep money you can get to. You should know how to strike a pose, curse like a sailor, kick like a mule and scream out your brother's name, though he may be three thousand miles away. And you mustn't be a fool.'

*

Elsewhere, it is not desolate Mexico, it is gentle Cumbria in England, in the hours well beyond midnight. Harriet Martineau is to be found heading up the Kirkstone road to Pelter Bridge, under a black sky leaking light. She is alone, but hasn't composed a note-to-self to keep her spirits up. She is one of a group of people I guided into the closing pages of *The Indigo Hours* – the place to be if your walk takes you out of darkness and into approaching dawn.

Walking into light cheers W.H. Hudson as he heads for Stonehenge, and his senses revitalise. There are new sights before him ('the rose and purple sky') and the inevitable sounds ('a tawny owl began to hoot'); and then the sounds of a tinkling bell are heard, a cyclist, also heading for the stones. Though it's better to come by foot of course, to get closer to the awakening world around, with fewer of its delights missed out on.

As for other dawn types: they tell us that the walk into light transforms their behaviour – again. The light will bring a self-reckoning; the light will bring a sense of guilt (if you've been out carousing the night before); and, at best, the light will bring an appetite for the day ahead, which is essential 'for our well-being', as suggested by one person gazing eastwards. Hard edges and true colours will return, ditto familiar smells and sounds, and the touch of something strange is forgotten now.

Soon to leave the stage are the watchmen and squabblers, the dingbats and street kids. Until, that is, the light fades and darkness falls, and it's time to find the blues once more.

W. G. SEBALD

– The Curtain Rises –

The rain clouds had dispersed when, after dinner, I took my first walk around the streets and lanes of the town. Darkness was falling, and only the lighthouse with its shining glass cabin still caught the last luminous rays that came in from the western horizon. Footsore and weary as I was, I sat down on a bench on the green called Gunhill and looked out on the tranquil sea, from the depths of which the shadows were now rising. Everyone who had been out on an evening stroll was gone. I felt as if I were in a deserted theatre, and I should not have been surprised if a curtain had suddenly risen before me and on the proscenium I had beheld. . .

From *The Rings of Saturn*, 1995,
translated by Michael Hulse, 1998

– The Stage is Set –

The village transformation is described in theatrical terms, since the square after sunset becomes the centre of life, and has an absurd resemblance to a stage-setting.

One side of this square is bounded by the weather-beaten front of the posting-inn. The stone terrace before this impressive dwelling forms the proscenium where, after dinner, the spectators assemble. To the right of the square stands the pale pink 'Post and Telegraph Bureau.' Beyond is a mysterious yellowish house with an arched entrance. Facing these, on the left, are the *dépendance* of the inn, and the customhouse. In the left background, the village street is seen winding down, between houses that look like 'studies' in old-fashioned drawing-books to the bridge across the river and the first loops of the post-road over the village pass. Opposite the inn is the obligatory village fountain, and the rallying-point of the chorus. Snow peaks fill the background of the stage.

Dinner over, the eager spectators, hasten to the terrace. Already the orchestra is tuning its instruments, and the chorus, recruited from the hayfields, are gathering in the wings. A dozen of them straggle in and squat on the jutting stone basement of the post-office; others hang picturesquely about the fountain, or hover up the steep street, awaiting the prompter's call. Presently some of the subordinate characters stroll across the stage – the owner of the saw-mill, a tall man in homespun, deferentially saluted by the chorus; two personages in black coats, with walking-sticks, who always appear together; a gentleman of leisure, in a white cap with a visor, smoking a long cigar and attended by an inquisitive Pomeranian dog; a citizen in white socks and carpet slippers, giving his arm to his wife, and preceded by a little boy with a green butterfly-box over his shoulder; then the gold-braided customhouse officer hurrying up late for his cue; two or three local ladies in sunburnt millinery and spectacles, who drop in to see the postmistress; and a showy young man, with the look of having seen life, emerges from the post-office conspicuously reading a letter, to the undisguised interest of the chorus, the ladies and the Pomeranian. As these figures pass and repass in a kind of social silence, they suggest the leisurely opening of some play peopled by types with generic names – the Innkeeper, the Postmistress, the Syndic – some comedy of Goldoni's, perhaps, but void of Goldoni's simple malice.

Meanwhile the porter has lit the oil-lanterns hanging by a chain over the door of the inn; a celestial hand has performed a similar office for the evening star above the peaks; and through the hush that has settled on the square comes a distant sound of bells . . . Instantly the action begins; the innkeeper appears, supported by the porter and the waiter; a wave of acclamation runs through the chorus; and the Pomeranian trots down the road.

The preposterous yellow coach – a landau attached to a glass 'clarence'– crosses the cobble-paved stage, swinging round with a grand curve to the inn door. Vague figures, detaching themselves from the chorus, flit about; the two blackcoats, critically aloof, lean on their sticks to watch the scene; and the Pomeranian bustles. Here they come, familiar as the figures in a Noah's ark: Germans first – the little triple-chinned man with a dachshund, out of 'Fliegende Blätter'; the slippered Hercules with a face like that at the end of a meerschaum pipe, and their sentimental females; shrill and vivid Italians; a pleasant pig-faced priest. Also Americans going 'right through,' with their city and state writ large upon their luggage; English girls like navvies, and some Frenchmen like girls. The arched doorway absorbs them all.

Another jingle of bells and a flash of lamps on the bridge proclaim that a second coach is coming. The same ceremony repeats itself; and another detachment of the travelling menagerie descends. This time there is a family of rodents, who look as though they ought to be enclosed in wire netting and judiciously nourished on lettuce; there is a small fierce man in knickerbockers and a sash, conducting a large submissive wife; there is an unfortunate lady in spectacles, who looks like one of the Creator's rejected experiments, and carries a grey linen bag embroidered with forget-me-nots. And of course there is the inevitable youth in walking boots with alpenstock, who sends home a bunch of edelweiss to his awestruck family . . . These, too, disappear.

Only one spectator lingers. A thoughtful man in a snuff-coloured overcoat, who gives the measure of the social resources of the village by the deliberate way in which, evening after evening, he strolls around the empty coaches, looks into their windows, examines the wheels and poles, and then mournfully moves off into the darkness.

From *Italian Backgrounds*, 1905

VERNON LEE

– With Moving Blobs –

A hidden sunset was going on when I reached the top of the rock. I walked up and down, in and out of the desecrated abbey church, choked with dusty scaffoldings inside, and barricaded outside with unused cranes and trolleys; and, for all this desecration of supposed repair, mouldy and green with damp. In front, below, stretched miles of grey sands to an invisible sea; and over them hung a pall of leaden clouds with ladders of pale-grey beams. The tourists were at dinner in the various Poulard inns; and the only living sound was the screech of greedy seagulls round the rock. Rarely in all my life has any place filled me with such overwhelming sadness and desire to rush away.

Descending from the Abbey, and skirting the little churchyard, I stumbled upon a little half-hidden church, and entered. It was dark, irregularly spotted with candlelight for service, and unseen women were chanting a litany. A church, I imagine, quite modern and trivial; but in that darkness, only the altar blazing, with a vague sheen of gold from the procession banners hanging all round, and with the scanty, scarce visible, congregation bending over the prie-dieu, it might have been of any time; and it made me realise, with reverence and tenderness, the reality of this place of mediaeval pilgrimage, this sanctuary, girt with quicksands, of 'Saint Michael in the Peril of the Sea,' to whom Roland commended his soul when he perished. This put me in conceit with Mont-Saint-Michel, and made me a little indignant with myself. What! – I had wanted a place of pilgrimage for my own private delectation, strictly without pilgrims, or at best only ghostly pilgrims made for myself! Fie upon such superfineness! Mankind is always vulgar, for vulgarity is mere misapplication of its energies, or perhaps misapplication of our squeamishness; and without mankind, vulgarity and all, no Mont-Saint-Michel and no me to cavil about it. The Canterbury pilgrims, judging by some of the stories they related, were vulgar; the pilgrims to Eleusis, from words dropped by Aristophanes, were even vulgarer; and there is considerable lack of dignity and sweetness in the crowd of ladies celebrating the entombment of Adonis, in the account left by Theocritus. And are not tourists the modern and lay representatives of pilgrims, starting on their journey, however much they yell on the brakes and squabble for Mme Poulard Aine's omelette, with desires of spiritual improvement and vague, unwonted feelings of romance?

Later, this more humane attitude of mind allowed me to take a certain pleasure in watching from the little garden gate the bands of tourists strolling from the eating-houses to their various resting-places. Moving blobs of Japanese lanterns, red and orange and green, and yellow lights and grotesque shadows proceeding along the old wooden house fronts, and across the turrets and battlements, with snatches of comic songs and goblin laughter. Thus, no doubt, the rollicking pilgrims of old, for whom the abbey was built, and the great vaulted and pillared refectories and foresteries.

From 'Mont-Saint-Michel', in *The Enchanted Woods*, 1905

EDWARD LEAR

– Between Civility and Morpheus –

Leaving the dry riverbed we climbed the second ridge, and descended to another fiumara, which runs to the sea below Amendolia, a castellated but deserted town, halfway up to the skies, as it were, and yet far below Bova. Here we entered the Distretto di Gerace, and were ordered to halt by some gendarmes, who came from a hut and inspected our passports, after which delay we began to climb the ascent to Bova in earnest, and for many an hour. But still we wearily worked on, and up. Bova seemed always like the phantom bark – never the nearer. We had long passed the level of the Castle of Amendolia, and were looking down into its empty courts, yet the unattainable peak was still far above us – and truly magnificent was the view, looking back from the points of rock where we frequently halted to rest, after passing the thick oak woods which encircle Bova. With these objects below our feet, the immense perspective of diminishing lines and torrents, finished by the complete and simple outline of Etna beyond the sea, is certainly one of the finest scenes to be found in beautiful Italy, even in the waning light. While drawing it, numerous groups of picturesque peasants passed us, on their return homewards, and almost all stopped and offered pears, in the most good-natured way possible. After a last hard climb, we arrived at Bova, as the dusk had made all things dark and alike, and we were unable to perceive 'what like' was the palazzo of Don Antonio Marzano. He, with his wife, received us with the greatest hospitality, on reading the recommendatory letter furnished to us by Don Antonio da Nava. But the greatest penance of this roving life is the state of exhaustion and weariness in which you arrive at your evening abode; and yet you feel obliged to play the part for a certain time to your entertainers. The wrestling between a sense of duty and an oppressive inclination to sleep is most painful. The good people, too, persist in delaying supper (in order that they may provide a great one) till you are reduced (ere it comes . . .) to a state of torture and despair, in the protracted struggle between hunger and civility and Morpheus.

From *Journals of a Landscape Painter in Southern Calabria*, 1852

LESLIE STEPHEN

– The Wrong Way at 7.30 p.m. –

We were now on known ground. Nothing but a level stretch of glacier intervened. The Eggischhorn inn began to paint itself distinctly on our imaginations, but we were hardly likely to reach the Eggischhorn before dark. I therefore objected to any unnecessary halts, and after taking a standing meal and abandoning our ladder to the tender mercies of the glacier, we started at a rapid pace for our much-desired haven. We passed a wilderness of boulders and mossy slopes, where a few wretched sheep pick up a mysterious existence above the glacier, then descended the waterfall, and after a rapid march found ourselves at 7.30 p.m. at the point where the stream from the Marjelen See descends beneath the ice close to a few isolated huts. We were all rather tired. We were disposed to look upon our day's work as done, and we hardly relished another climb. Still we were afraid to take the lower path to the Eggischhorn, and preferred ascending the stream to the Marjelen Alp, hoping to find locals there if it should be too dark to see the path to the inn. We climbed wearily and slowly upwards, halting to take an occasional pull at the stream and to imbibe certain remnants of brandy. Gradually it became very dark. We were guided chiefly by the sound of the rushing water on our left. Every form of mountain and rock had become indistinct in the twilight, and then blotted out in a drizzling mist. The stream seemed to be falling from an indefinite height out of absolute darkness, and the path refused to bend over into the little plain by the lake. We might be climbing right up to the top of the Grat, when at length we reached a small hummock of rock, on which was planted something like a wooden cross. We halted and looked round. Nothing but a mixture of mist and night was to be seen. Someone raised a despairing yodel on the chance that we were near the chalets. No answer. Another louder yell, in which we all joined; silence again, and then, to our intense delight, something like a faint reply. A general yell now produced a singular phenomenon. A faint spark appeared at an indefinite distance, indistinctly glistening through the drizzle. The spark grew larger, began to move, and presently came rushing in a straight line towards us. On approaching, a boy was discovered attached to one end of a flaming piece of pine wood. He had come on our cries from the Marjelen Alp, and guided us back to it, a distance of two or three hundred yards. This piece of luck raised our spirits. We soon became valiant over warm milk and bread, and therefore having changed our prospect of lodging in damp rhododendron beds for the certainty of dry straw under a roof, began to think whether better things might not be done. Should we try to reach the Eggischhorn? The guides pooh-poohed the idea. Liveing, who had been rather unwell a day or two before, signified his opinion by taking off his boots and lying composedly down on the regulation mixture of hay and fleas. I was for giving in to the majority; but the strongest and most obstinate member of the party showed at once his courage and the vigour of his appetite by insisting upon making a dash for supper at the Eggischhorn. A little diplomacy was therefore used. Certain hints at five francs produced a willingness on the part of the small Will-o'-the-wisp to go in any direction we might please to mention. The guides grumbled emphatically. A variety of judicious appeals to their skill, and our extreme confidence in it, at last induced them to take a more favourable view of the case. The construction of a lantern out of an empty bottle and a candle removed one objection which had been strongly urged. The right plan, I may remark, is to strike out the bottom of the bottle and to insert the candle through the neck with the wick foremost. The glass of the bottle then forms a satisfactory screen. As an additional and (as I proved) more effective source of light, the boy constructed a torch by splitting one end of a large piece of wood with an axe, and inserting splinters of wood into the splits. These when lighted made a grand blaze, and we all started in high spirits for the inn. Liveing, animated by our example, sprang up and accompanied us.

For a time all went right enough. The torch led the van, and the lantern brought up the rear. We climbed the crest of the hill leading towards the Eggischhorn rapidly and successfully.

'We shall have supper before 11 o'clock,' said Hardy. Presently the torch went out. It was relighted, and we were off again. Soon, however, our progress, which had been straightforward, seemed to me to be rather wandering. 'We have just missed the path,' the boy explained, 'but we shall find it again directly.' It became doubtful, however, whether we were not looking for it in the wrong direction. Shortly afterwards a discussion arose – whether the narrow gully which we were descending was not the very one we had come up ten minutes before. During the discussion the torch went out. In attempting to relight it we put the candle out. Then all the matches were wet through, and it was not till we had hunted to the bottom of someone's knapsack that we found any that would work. At last we succeeded; and, to save trouble, I may say that this process of extinction of all our lights, followed by their laborious rekindling, went on at continually shorter intervals till we seemed to be sitting down longer than we were walking. Meanwhile the search for the missing path seemed every moment more hopeless. After scrambling up and down, and round and round for a long time, we found ourselves in a disconsolate and bewildered state of mind, standing on a damp ledge of grass at the foot of a big rock staring vacantly into blank darkness. Whether to go up or down, or right or left, we knew no more than if we had been suddenly dropped into the middle of the great Sahara. There was only one thing for it. We took our knapsacks and put on our remaining articles of dress, e.g., two pairs of socks, an extra pair of trousers, a flannel shirt, a waistcoat, and a dozen paper shirt-collars, and crouched down under the rock, hoping that the wind would keep in the right quarter, that the puddle in which we were sitting would be speedily absorbed, and that the sun would get up as early as possible. The guides made some very sarcastic remarks, in very broad patois, about gentlemen who wouldn't take advice, and I refrained from allusions to supper. The boy who had attempted to guide us had meanwhile vanished into the depths of the night. At this instant, just as I had drawn my second pair of trousers over my second flannel shirt, he suddenly emerged from the dark, exclaiming, 'I've found a man!' It struck me as a bewildering and improbable circumstance; and I did not at first appreciate the fact that he was referring to a stone man or cairn, marking the route to the Eggischhorn! In a few seconds the whole party was under way again, not even halting to take off the extra apparel. A dreary and a dismal walk we had.

In front was the boy with the torch. At short intervals halts had to be called, to coax the said torch by various means into renewed activity. In the intervals between these halts, I, being about fifth in the line, was only conscious of the torch as a kind of halo spreading out a short way and mistily on either side of certain black bodies, which oscillated strangely between me and it. From these black masses came sounds expressive of revolutionary sentiments about hills and stones in general, and the Eggischhorn in particular. My radius of vision included about a yard of hill, inclining at a very steep angle to my left, scattered with mysterious objects, which generally turned out to be deep holes when I thought they were stones, and very unsteady and sharp-edged stones when I thought they were puddles. Stumbling, groaning, slipping, and pulling up short over stones, puddles, slippery grass, and every variety of pitfall, including cows, we pushed wearily on, and soon became conscious that we were on a thing that called itself a path.

A few minutes at a quicker pace, and the Eggischhorn inn appeared. A wild yell from four weary, hungry, and thirsty travellers roused M. Wellig to a sense of his duties, and later on said travellers were asleep, with two good bottles of champagne inside them.

From *The Playground of Europe*, 1909

HERMAN MELVILLE

– Lanterns, Assassins, Impressions –

Beautiful moonlight . . . Under a clear night, stars shining with brilliancy! Walking the lane. Stopped. The intermingling of a dark tree with a lighted spire was expressive of the intermingling of life and death . . . And last night was very pleasant; walked the deck with the German Mr Adler, till a late hour, and talked about 'fixed fate' and 'free will' . . .

*

Wet underfoot. The showers at night were like our June showers. Walked on top of the house . . . The dark and dangerous streets of Constantinople carry thoughts of assassination; staid in all night . . . Dangerous going out, owing to footpads and assassins. The curse of these places. Can't go out at night, no places to go to, even if you could . . . Cries of watchmen at night. Lanterns. Assassins . . . Walked under the Arcades in the night time . . . At night. Fighting of the dogs. Strange to come upon a pack of them in some lonely lane. Mostly yellow, with long sharp noses . . . Wandering about came across Black Hole in the street. Did not enter far . . . I strolled about, and it being Saturday night entertained myself by vagabonding through the courts and lanes and looking in at the windows.

*

Streets very lively at night . . . Walked by moonlight and gaslight in piazza. Numbers of singers & musicians. The tumblers and comic actors in the open space near Rialto. The expression of the Women Tumblers! . . . Walked about. Then a Café . . . At night walked to the Café Greco. Dense smoke. Rowdy looking chaps . . . Stopped at a beer shop and took a black ale in a comical flagon . . . I came away and walking to The Cock Inn drank a glass of Stout and headed home to bed . . . Into a dark and rainy night, and made my way across the Pont (within a biscuit's toss of the Morgue) to my sixth story apartment. I don't like that mystic door leading out of the closet.

From *Journal of a Visit to London and the Continent*, 1849–1850;
Journal Up The Straits, 1856–1857;
Journal of a Visit to Europe and to The Levant, 1856–1857

HENRY DAVID THOREAU

– The Dark is Medicinal –

Many walk by day; few walk by night. It is a very different season. On all sides novelties present themselves. Instead of the sun there are the moon and stars, instead of the wood-thrush there is the whip-poor-will, instead of butterflies in the meadows, fire-flies, winged sparks of fire! Who would have believed it? On our open river terraces they appear to occupy the ground like an army – their heads nodding in the breeze. Small trees and shrubs are seen in the midst, overwhelmed as by an inundation. Then, the shadows of rocks and trees, and shrubs and hills, are more conspicuous than the objects themselves. The slightest irregularities in the ground are revealed by the shadows, and what the feet find smooth, appears rough and diversified in consequence. For the same reason the whole landscape is more variegated and picturesque than by day. The smallest recesses in the rocks are dim and cavernous; the ferns in the wood appear of tropical size. The sweet fern and indigo in overgrown wood-paths wet you with dew up to your middle. A distant cliff looks like a phosphorescent space on a hillside. The woods are heavy and dark. Nature slumbers. You see the moonlight reflected from particular stumps in the recesses of the forest, as if she selected what to shine on. These small fractions of her light remind one of a plant called moon-seed – as if the moon were sowing it in such places. In the night the eyes are partly closed or retire into the head. So other senses take the lead. The walker is guided as well by the sense of smell. Every plant and field and forest emits its odour now, swamp-pink in the meadow and tansy in the road; and there is the peculiar dry scent of corn which has begun to show its tassels. The senses both of hearing and smelling are more alert. We hear the tinkling of rills which we never detected before. From time to time, high up on the sides of hills, you pass through a stratum of warm air. A blast which has come up from the sultry plains of noon. It circulates about from wood-side to hill-side like a dog that has lost its master, now that the sun is gone. The rocks retain all night the warmth of the sun which they have absorbed. And so does the sand – if you dig a few inches into it you will find a warm bed.

How insupportable would be the days, if the night with its dews and darkness did not come to restore the drooping world. As the shades begin to gather around us, our primeval instincts are aroused, and we steal forth from our lairs, like the inhabitants of the jungle, in search of those silent and brooding thoughts which are the natural prey of the intellect. There are nights in this climate of such serene beauty, so medicinal and fertilising to the spirit, that methinks a sensitive nature would not devote them to oblivion, and perhaps there is no man who would not be better and wiser for spending them out of doors, though he should sleep all the next day to pay for it; should sleep an Endymion sleep, as the ancients expressed it – nights which warrant the Grecian epithet ambrosial, when the atmosphere is charged with dewy fragrance, and with music, and we take our repose and have our dreams awake – when the moon is not secondary to the sun and

'gives us his blaze again,
Void of its flame, and sheds a softer day.
Now through the passing cloud she seems to stoop,
Now up the pure cerulean rides sublime.'

From *Night and Moonlight*, 1863

Different Shades of Dark

'The colour of the landscape changes hourly, growing ever more and more harmonious. At sunset we have watched it change from glistening pink, to magnificent purple, then to silvery mauve. Finally at the onset of night to pure transparent blue.'
– George Sand

'At the moment we are all convinced this blue and violet evening must exist somewhere; and in some way, forever, in the world, or in the mind of God.'
– Claudio Magris

'The sky has turned a deep slate blue, identical with the blue that now washes the bare lower stretches of the mountains.' – Nan Shepherd

'If I were to give details it would seem like colour run mad. Such purple velvet, as are worn by the mountains and clouds, are fresh wonders to me every night.' – Bayard Taylor

'To the south I can see a thin streak of violet and cobalt sky stretching across eighty degrees of the horizon. The pervasive light here is the milky blue of the reflected moon.' – Barry Lopez

'I am always happy when I can take a solitary walk at night. How soothing it is to let the eyes rest on the deep deep blue of the sky, and also of the sea.'
– Marie Bashkirtseff

'It often seems to me that the dark is more richly coloured than the day, having hues of the most intense violets and blues.' – Vincent van Gogh

'Summer night, and blue lightning.' – Hermann Hesse

'The path was pitted with hard-edged shadows that I'd never noticed in daylight, more reminiscent of the surface of the moon.' – Nicholas Shakespeare

'The sky is a soft tiffany blue, darker above us, and there's not a breath of wind . . . and the paths become luminous trails through the darkness.'
– Helen McDonald

'Having come to a stop and drunk a few glasses of water, I lay quietly down in front of a door, and while looking into the deep azure of the sky I was not long in sinking into a deep sleep, just as if I were lying on the softest of beds. Never did a lovelier and more serene night robe the earth in its blue velvet mantle.' – Théophile Gautier

MARY MORRIS

– It's Only Nine O'clock –

I was on my own. I had no idea what to do with myself. It grew dark early and I wasn't ready for bed. Instead I went out for a walk. The streets were dark and cobbled and smelled of garbage. I didn't know my way as I wandered through the back alleys and narrow roads. I passed restaurants with crowded tables and lighted rooms where families stared into the blue light of miniature TVs. Old women grasping babies, sat telling stories and laughing on doorsteps. I searched for a movie house, a coffee shop with guitar music, but all I found were dozens of bars filled with men, and I wasn't ready to go into one alone.

I walked to the center of town, to a square lined with benches and trees, which in most parts of Mexico is called the *zócalo*, but in San Miguel is called the *jardín*, where an odd procession passed in front of me. A circle of girls walked in the clockwise direction around the perimeters of the *jardín*, perhaps half the distance of a square city block. There were at least a hundred of them. And encircling them, moving counterclockwise, was a group of young men. Hesitating, I cut through their circle and sat down on a bench, where I watched as the single men and women of the town encircle each other on and on into the darkness in this ritualised form of courtship – called the promenade – which would occur every night at the hour when the birds came home to rest in the trees of the *jardín*.

They flirted and giggled and pretended to ignore one another, but as darkness fell, some wandered off, boy leading girl away to a more secluded spot in a darkened street, an alleyway. I imagined them whispering each other's names and thought of how far I was from someone who might whisper mine.

The church bells rang. From the steeple clock that seemed to rule over this town and mark the monotony of the days, I saw that it was only nine o'clock. I still had much of the evening ahead of me and no place to go. Then I noticed people entering church. Toothless old men and corpulent women with babies wrapped in shawls shuffled in. Girls in miniskirts and white blouses held the hands of boys in green or cranberry polyester pants, others in blue jeans, black hair slicked back, lingered in the alcoves.

In this town of shrieking birds and promenading lovers, I could think of nothing else to do, so I went to church. I walked hesitantly into the large Gothic stone building and down an aisle toward the apse . . .

I took it all in, and then I walked home. I descended the hill, toward the bus stop, until I reached the turnoff for San Antonio. At the turnoff is the dirt road, about a quarter of a mile long . . .

For the first time, I walked that quarter of a mile at night alone. Every shadow, every sound made me turn. I behaved like a hunted thing. It is not easy to move though the world alone, and it is never easy for a woman. You must keep your wits about you. You mustn't get yourself into dark places you can't get out of. Keep money you can get to, an exit behind you, and some language at your fingertips. You should know how to strike a pose, curse like a sailor, kick like a mule, and scream out your brother's name, though he may be three thousand miles away. And you mustn't be a fool.

From *Nothing to Declare: Memoirs of a Woman Travelling Alone*, 1988

CAROL LAKE

– The Moon Shines Bright on Charlie Chaplin –

By the time we leave the fairground we look thoroughly disreputable: the quilted bottoms of Zarina's pyjamas are covered in mud, my hair has escaped its grips, and Shamuna has lost a shoe in the mud.

'She says she doesn't care. *Isn't* she naughty?' Shamuna gives out a low chuckle, and kisses her bear. We sing 'Ten Green Bottles', and after that Zarina gives us 'Bobby Shaftoe', complete with handclaps.

The moon comes up behind the housetops as we walk home:

The moon shines bright on Charlie Chaplin,
His boots are cracking, his boots are cracking,
Oh, the moon shines bright on Charlie Chaplin,
Until they send him to the Dardanelles.

We sing our way home; the moon rises up at the end of the street, shining straight into our path, big and silver, and very close to the earth.

From *Rosehill*, 1989

CHRISTIANE RITTER

– The Extinction of All Colours –

We make the door fast and start back with heavy hearts because we have still found no game. It is night and frightfully cold. The sky is almost completely clouded. In the north the low red sun shines through tattered shrouds of mist. Its rays spread a livid light over the hills of Reindeer-land, vanishing into the milky light of the snow. From the north comes the surging sounds of the sea in the open spaces among the ice. We quicken our pace; we do not want to be caught on the ice by fog and snow, for we have not brought a compass with us.

It is about midnight when we reach the fjord. It is grey, and covered with a damp and icy mist. We follow the tracks we left by our skis when we came here, while the air begins to get thicker and thicker. The sun grows a deep copper red, and the peculiar atmosphere, which is met with only in the north, and in the Arctic, envelops us, the indeterminateness of day and night, light and darkness, the extinction of all colours and outlines.

I have to call up all my energy to keep up a quick, even pace. My feet are aching with cold. My leather shoes were thawed but not dried in the warmth of

Sven's hut, and now they are frozen stone hard . . . Although I drank so much coffee, I am again tortured by thirst.

'Don't eat snow,' Hermann calls out to me. 'It makes you tired and still more thirsty. You'll have to control yourself.'

The sky grows darker and a grey mist encloses us; the soft snowflakes begin to fall. If a wind should rise, obliterating our ski tracks, we shall be lost on the ice. My feet have grown quite numb, and for the first time I feel the full pitilessness of the Arctic world. Now I can understand the patience and the prudence of the hunters, their obedience to nature, their unconditional submission to its laws. Only in that way can they keep themselves alive, in their solitariness, through all the dangers of the land.

My husband goes ahead of me and does not speak. I know that if he were alone he would go more quickly, to avoid the fog and snow on the ice. We can no longer see the mainland. The heavy damp air makes breathing difficult, and my limbs feel like lead. Judging from the bear tracks, we are about in the middle of the fiord. There do not seem to be any new tracks, and the old ones are almost obliterated by snow. Everything else is submerged in my weariness and apathy. I can scarcely keep my thirst under control.

Hermann amazes me. He does not feel thirsty; he steps out vigorously, turning round now and again to smile at me patiently. For him the trip is scarcely an exertion at all.

I do not know how many hours we have been on our way when the mists begin slowly to thin, and out of its dense veils rise the mountaintops of Bock Bay and Cape Roos to the south of the fiord . . . The blue sky arches above them. We have reached the fair-weather zone of Grey Hook, the triumphant, clear ice atmosphere, further from the sea. The familiar Rillenberg Range comes nearer and grows larger. And on the flat foreland, a tiny black point, our beloved little hut. We seem to be still an eternity away from it when we make a surprising discovery.

Beside the ski tracks we made in the morning there are fresh bear tracks leading towards the hut. A bear returning from the end of the fiord seems to have taken an interest in our tracks. We can see how he has padded along beside them, and with his forepaws thoughtfully shuffled the snow to and fro across the tracks.

'It will be by our hut,' Hermann cries out, his eyes sparkling, and involuntarily he accelerates his pace. I am too tired to be glad or fearful; my only thought is that the bear may delay my going to bed.

From *A Woman in the Polar Night*, 1938,
translated by Jane Degras, 1954

JOHANN PAUL FRIEDRICH RICHTER

– Starlight Parties –

This place is a moonlight Eden for us drift-ice people. Because here we find the living fulfilment of the youthful dream of nights spent wandering or singing. But I asked why the people only walked and sang in the streets like ill-humoured night watchmen, instead of having entire evening-star and morning-star parties assemble? And why not have a colourful procession – for every soul was in love – roaming through the magnificent arbors and the brightest moonlit meadows of flowers; and then to contribute to such joy with two phrases on the flute – namely, the double-ended lengthening of the brief night by sunset and sunrise, and the allied twilights of dusk and dawn.

Undated letter

– Hootings –

We walked first on our own path. It was a silent night. The stars were out by ones and twos, but no cuckoo, no little birds. The air was not warm, and we have observed since Tuesday, 8th, when William wrote, 'The sun has long been set,' that we have no birds singing after the evening is set in. We walked to our new view of Rydale, but it put on a sullen face. There was an owl hooting in Bainrigg's. Its first halloo was so like a human shout that I was surprised, when it gave its second call tremulous and lengthened out, to find that the shout had come from an owl. The full moon (not quite full) was among a company of shady island clouds. William observed that the full moon, above a dark fir grove, is a fine image of the descent of a superior being. There was a shower which drove us into John's Grove before we had quitted our favourite path. We walked upon John's path before we went to view Rydale . . .

William wrote to Mary and Sara about The Leech Gatherer and wrote to both of them in one . . . and to Coleridge also . . . I walked with William . . . on our own path. We were driven away by the horses that go on the commons; then we went to look at Rydale; walked a little in the fir grove; the owls hooted; went again to the top of the hill, and came home. A mild and sweet night. William stayed behind me. I threw him the cloak out of the window. The moon overcast. He sat a few minutes in the orchard; came in sleepy, and hurried to bed. I carried him his bread and butter.

A sweet grey, mild morning. The birds sing soft and low. William has not slept all night; it wants only ten minutes of ten, and he is in bed yet. After William rose we went and sate in the orchard till dinner time. We walked a long time in the evening upon our favourite path; the owls hooted, the night hawk sang to itself incessantly, but there were no little birds, no thrushes. I left William writing a few lines about the night hawk and other images of the night, and went to seek for letters.

From *The Journals of Dorothy Wordsworth*, 1897

RICHARD JEFFERIES

– 'Ching Ching' and 'Twit Twit' –

The gloom of short January is settling down fast in the wood. The silent and motionless trees rise out of a mysterious shadow, which fills up the spaces between their trunks. Only above, where their delicate outer branches are shown against the dark sky, is there any separation between them. Somewhere in the deep shadow of the underwood a blackbird calls 'ching, ching' before he finally settles himself to roost. In the yew the lesser birds are already quiet, sheltered by the evergreen spray; they have also sought the ivy-grown trunks. 'Twit, twit,' sounds high overhead as one or two belated little creatures, scarcely visible, pass quickly for the cover of the furze on the hill. The short January evening is but of a few minutes' duration; just now it was only dusky, and already the interior of the wood is impenetrable to the glance. There rises a loud though distant clamour of rooks and daws, who have moved in their roost-trees. Darkness is almost on them, yet they cannot quite settle. The cawing and dawing rises to a pitch, and then declines. The wood is silent and it is suddenly night.

From *The Life of The Fields*, 1884

JOHN MUIR

– All Manner of Sounds –

When I was in the trackless woods, the great mysterious night becoming more mysterious in the thickening darkness, I gave up hope of finding food or a house bed, and searched for a dry spot on which to sleep safely. I walked rapidly for hours in the wet, level woods, but not a foot of dry ground could I find. Hollow-voiced owls were calling without intermission. All manner of night sounds came from strange insects and beasts, one by one, or crowded together. All had a home, but I. I came to an open place where pines grew and thought now at last I would find dry ground. But even the sandy barren was wet, and I had to grope in the dark a long time, feeling the ground with my hands when my feet ceased to plash, before I at last discovered a little hillock dry enough to lie down on. I ate a piece of bread that fortunately I had in my bag, drank some of the brown water about my precious hillock, and lay down. The noisiest of the unseen witnesses around me were the owls, who pronounced their gloomy speeches with profound emphasis, but did not prevent the coming of sleep to heal the weariness.

From *A Thousand-Mile Walk to the Gulf*, 1916

GEORGE ORWELL

– The Stars are a Free Show –

Bozo seemed an interesting man. I went down to the Embankment to meet him. We walked down into Lambeth. Bozo limped slowly, with a queer crablike gait, half sideways, dragging his smashed foot behind him. As we were crossing the bridge he stopped in one of the alcoves to rest. He fell silent for a minute or two, and to my surprise I saw that he was looking at the stars. He touched my arm and pointed to the sky with his stick.

'Say, will you look at Aldebaran! Look at the colour. Like a great blood orange!'

From the way he spoke he might have been an art critic in a picture gallery. I was astonished. I confessed that I did not know which Aldebaran was – indeed, I had never even noticed that the stars were of different colours. Bozo began to give me some elementary hints on astronomy, pointing out the chief constellations. He seemed concerned at my ignorance. I said to him surprised:

'You seem to know a lot about stars.'

'Not a great lot. I know a bit, though. I got two letters from the Astronomer Royal thanking me for writing about meteors. Now and again I walk at night and watch for meteors. The stars are a free show; it don't cost anything to use your eyes.'

'What a good idea! I should never have thought of it.'

'Well, you got to take an interest in something. It don't follow that because a man's on the road he can't think of anything but tea-and-two-slices.'

From *Down and Out in Paris and London*, 1933

More Stars

'I want to be out under the stars – where there is lots of room.' – Georgia O'Keefe

'The stars have caused me to pause in the middle of my walk.' – Barry Lopez

'The road was perfectly quiet and lonely and I did not meet a soul. The night was magnificent and frosty, very cold and sparkling keen with stars. And I saw two meteors.' – Francis Kilvert

'We remained in the woods during the day, and as soon as darkness overshadowed the earth, we started again on our gloomy way, having no guide but the North Star. We continued to walk by night, and secrete ourselves in the woods by day; and every night, before emerging from our hiding-place, we would anxiously look for our best friend and leader – the North Star.' – William W. Brown

'You speculate on the height of the starry canopy. The stars are the jewels of the night, and surpass anything which day has to show.'
– Henry David Thoreau

'After having waited so long, I thought I might venture to speak to her. Inspired by the soft influence of the stars, and by the powerful wish to make an impression on this lovely woman – after having gently coughed, to warn her, and to soften the sound of my voice – in the most affectionate manner I said: "It is very fine tonight."' – Xavier de Maistre

'So you went with me as I was walking out tonight. We looked at the stars, and they were different. All the constellations were different, and I, who was looking for Orion, to show you, because he is rising now, was very puzzled by these thick, close, brilliant new constellations Then suddenly we saw one planet, so beautiful, a large, fearful, strong star, that we were both pierced by it, possessed, for a second. Then I said, "That's Jupiter" – but I felt that it wasn't Jupiter – at least not the everyday Jupiter. Ask Jung or Freud about it? Never! It was a star that blazed for a second on one's soul.' – D. H. Lawrence

'Feeling oneself "pure and ready to see the stars" nothing is better than to climb up to the head of that stone known as the tower of the Seraskerat. If Satan should wish again to tempt anyone with the offer of all the kingdoms of the earth, he'd be sure of success were he to bring his victim up here.'
– Edmondo De Amicis

‘Gaze at the circling moon and stars, and guess their direction.’ – Hermann Hesse

‘One night I decided to listen to some music and put Eric Satie into the cassette. But the noise sounded alien, incongruous, so I turned if off and sucked on the whisky bottle instead. I talked to myself, rolling the names of the stars around on my tongue. Good-night Aldebaran. See you Sirius. Adios Corvus. I was glad there was a crow in the heavens.’
– Robyn Davidson

‘That night I fell asleep quickly. Only once, waking, I drank two ice-cold mouthfuls of water from my can and, leaning back, saw the Milky Way astonishingly bright through the pine tops, and felt something indescribable – like falling upwards into someone’s arms.’ – Richard Holmes

JOANNA KAVENNA

– We Are Made of Stardust –

I saw a black shadow ahead of me, its shape indeterminate. I thought it might be a refuge, somewhere warm and comfortable. A fire, a bed. I started hurrying forwards, but it became swiftly apparent it was just a ruin. The crumbling walls provided some shelter, so I lay down on the lee side. I was glad to be out of the wind. The sky was full of famous stars and layers of iridescent dust. I was reading a book by Hubert Reeves, *Pourquoi la nuit est-elle noire?* The dark night sky proves that the universe is finite. Also, we are made of stardust. When we die, this energy is dispersed into something else. Nothing that has existed can ever truly vanish. It made no sense. I was tired, my French wasn't good enough. The wind howled. I was asleep when someone tugged at my foot. I half-woke, assumed it was a dream. Black sky, celestial dust. I couldn't actually be sleeping in the depths of nowhere, alone. Then I heard a loud, definite rustling and then – worse – the sound of footsteps. Suddenly I was awake and very frightened. 'Who's there?' I said, stupidly. 'What do you want?' I said all sorts of stupid things and then with a desperate, trembling movement, I switched on the torch.

I expected – a murderer, a pale lunatic, a moon spirit, the ghost of my father. Instead – sheep! I was so angry with them, for scaring the hell out of me. But they looked miserable, with their little white faces. Like a Greek chorus, masked and anxious. I had stolen their bed. It was the only sheltered place for miles around. 'I'm sorry,' I said, still trembling from the shock. 'I'm only here for a night.' They stared at me, balefully. 'Why not settle down over there?' I said – gesturing towards the opposite wall. It wasn't as sheltered but it was better than nothing. For a while the sheep stood around, then by some mysterious consensus they gave up and wandered off. I switched off the torch, my heart still pounding. What a ridiculous scene! It took a while before I slept, if timorously, and when I woke again at dawn the sheep had vanished. I hoped they'd had a decent night.

From *Lost,* 2022

NICHOLAS SHAKESPEARE

– Sancho Takes on a Spectral Glimmer –

It's a whole other experience walking in the dark. To start with, it sounds different. A lion roars in the early morning because the noise carries that much more in the damp. At night, the sound of tyres on the road is muffled, as if absorbed by the darkness, and I need a torch to ward off the Ocado delivery van when, with no warning, it roars up our country lane in Wiltshire.

Taking Sancho for his last walk of the day, I am dragged at the dog's forceful pace into a black and white negative of my antemeridian world. Lights on in the houses that are lived in. The flashes of burglar alarms and big-screen TVs. I see other walkers out, with blinking miners-hats and wearing high-vis jackets. Walkers without torches, or unoccupied houses with window panes like empty eye sockets, become menacing.

Then the visibility factor. Ahead of me in the night somewhere, his golden contours lapped at and diminished by the winter gloom, Sancho takes on a spectral glimmer that reminds me not so much of the fast receding shape of my grandfather in one of his tearaway moods but a glow worm. Glow worms have died out in most places in England, surviving only on unimproved land. Patrolling this way and that at the end of his lead, Sancho sees me, but I frequently have no inkling where he is. He keeps disappearing, swallowed by the dark, and then re-appearing, like that small yellowish pulse of light I glimpsed one midnight on a disused railway track in Cumbria. He has no competition from overhead. This is Wiltshire in December 2020, there are no stars.

From *Lot's Wife, and Some Reflections on Walking at Night*, 2022

D. H. LAWRENCE

– Black, Black, Black –

No denying it was beautiful, with the oak-slopes and the wistfulness and the far-off feeling of loneliness. But I was in too great a temper to admit it. We clambered frenziedly to get warm, and the ice-heavy blue shadow fell over us all. The village began to send forth blue wood-smoke, and it seemed more than ever like the twilit West Country.

But thank you – we had to get back. And run the gauntlet of that stinking, stinking lane? Never. Towering with fury – quite unreasonable, but there you are – I marched the q-b down a declivity through a wood, over a ploughed field, along a cart-track, and so to the great highroad above the village and above the inn.

It was cold, and evening was falling into night. Down the highroad came wild half-ragged men on ponies, in all degrees of costume and not-costume: came four wide-eyed cows stepping down-hill round the corner, and three delicate, beautiful merino sheep which stared at us with their prominent, gold-curious eyes: came an ancient, ancient man with a stick: came a stout-chested peasant carrying a long wood-pole: came a straggle of alert and triumphant goats, long-horned, long-haired, jingling their bells.

Everybody greeted us hesitatingly. And everything came to a halt at the Risveglio corner, while the men had a nip.

I attacked the spotty-breast again.

Could I have milk?

No. Perhaps in an hour there would be milk. Perhaps not.

Was there anything to eat?

No – at half past seven there would be something to eat.

Was there a fire?

No – the man hadn't made the fire.

Nothing to do but to go to that foul bedroom or walk the highroad. We turned up the highroad again. Animals stood about the road in the frost-heavy air, with heads sunk passively, waiting for the men to finish their drinks in the beastly bar – we walked slowly up the hill. In a field on the right a flock of merino sheep moved mistily, uneasily, climbing at the gaps in the broken road bank, and sounding their innumerable small fine bells with a frosty ripple of sound. A figure which in the dark I had really thought was something inanimate broke into movement in the field.

It was an old shepherd, very old, in very ragged dirty black-and-white, who had been standing like a stone there in the open field-end for heaven knows how long, utterly motionless, leaning on his stick. Now he broke into a dream-motion and hobbled after the wistful, feminine, inquisitive sheep. The red was fading from the far-off west. At the corner, climbing slowly and wearily, we almost ran into a grey and lonely bull, who came stepping down-hill in his measured fashion like some god. He swerved his head and went round us.

We reached a place which we couldn't make out: then saw it was a cork-shed. There were stacks and stacks of cork-bark in the dusk, like crumpled hides.

'Now I'm going back,' said the q-b flatly, and she swung round. The last red was smouldering beyond the lost, thin-wooded hills of this interior. A fleece of blue, half-luminous smoke floated over the obscure village. The high-way wound downhill at our feet, pale and blue.

And the q-b was angry with me for my fury.

'Why are you so indignant! Anyone would think your moral self had been outraged! Why take it morally? You petrify that man at the inn by the very way you speak to him, such condemnation! Why don't you take it as it comes? It's all life.'

But no, my rage is black, black, black. Why, heaven knows. But I think it was because Sorgono had seemed so fascinating to me, when I imagined it beforehand. Oh so fascinating! If I had expected nothing I should not have been so hit. Blessed is he that expecteth nothing, for he shall not be disappointed.

*

In the bar a wretched candle was weeping light – uneasy, gloomy men were drinking their Saturday night-home-coming dram. Cattle lay down in the road, in the cold air as if hopeless.

Had the milk come?

No.

When would it come.

He didn't know.

Well, what were we to do? Was there no room? Was there nowhere where we could sit?

Yes, there was the stanza now.

Now!

Taking the only weed of a candle, and leaving the drinkers in the dark, he led us down a dark and stumbly earthen passage, over loose stones and an odd plank, as it would seem underground, to the stanza: the room.

The stanza! It was pitch dark – but suddenly I saw a big fire of oak-root, a brilliant, flamy, rich fire, and my rage in that second disappeared

From 'To Sorgono', *Sea and Sardinia,* 1921

LOREN EISELEY

– Towards the Streetlights –

Somewhere along a section of damp sand I encountered several large toads who were also making a night journey and who hopped along clumsily for a little way with me. There was something so attractive about their little bursts of energy that, tired as I was, I began to skip with them. I was delighted now to have even lowly company. First one would hop and then another, and I began to take my turn automatically with the rest. I do not know where they might have eventually led me, though I had a feeling that if I stayed and hopped with them long enough I might acquire this knowledge in some primordial manner.

With this thought I parted from them at a turn in the stream bed and made my way again over open rolling foothills in the dark. The land was rising. I was approaching the escarpment . . .

I met nothing living now except small twisted pines. Boulders swelled up from the turf like huge white puff balls . . . I reached the end of the escarpment and looked down.

The night lights of the city glistened in hundreds far out on the plain . . . Those faraway street lights beneath me were an irresistible attraction. They were the world I knew.

From 'Big Eyes and Small Eyes', *Gentry Magazine*, 1956

ROBERT LOUIS STEVENSON.

– Lighting the City –

Cities given, the problem was to light them. How to conduct individual citizens about the burgess-warren, once heaven had withdrawn its leading luminary? or – since we live in a scientific age – when once our spinning planet has turned its back upon the sun? The moon, from time to time, was doubtless very helpful; the stars had a cheery look among the chimney-pots; and a cresset here and there, on church or citadel, produced a fine pictorial effect, and, in places where the ground lay unevenly, held out the right hand of conduct to the benighted. But sun, moon, and stars abstracted or concealed, the night-faring inhabitant had to fall back – we speak on the authority of old prints – upon stable lanthorns, two stories in height. Many holes, drilled in the conical turret-roof of this vagabond Pharos, let up spouts of dazzlement into the bearer's eyes; and as he paced forth in the ghostly darkness, day and night swung to and fro and up and down about his footsteps. Blackness haunted his path; he was beleaguered by goblins as he went; and, curfew being struck, he found no light but that he travelled in throughout the township.

Closely following on this epoch of migratory

lanthorns in a world of extinction, came the era of oil-lights, hard to kindle, easy to extinguish, pale and wavering in the hour of their endurance. Rudely puffed the winds of heaven; roguishly clomb up the all-destructive urchin; and, lo! in a moment night re-established her void empire, and the cit groped along the wall, suppered but bedless, occult from guidance, and sorrily wading in the kennels. As if gamesome winds and gamesome youths were not sufficient, it was the habit to sling these feeble luminaries from house to house above the fairway! There, on invisible cordage, let them swing! And suppose some crane-necked general go speeding by on a tall charger, there would indubitably be some effusion of military blood, and oaths, and a certain crash of glass; and while the chieftain rode forward with a purple coxcomb, the street would be left to original darkness, unpiloted, unvoyageable, a province of the desert night. The conservative, looking before and after, draws from each contemplation the matter for content. Out of the age of gas lamps he glances back slightingly at the mirk and glimmer in which his ancestors wandered; his heart waxes jocund at the contrast; nor do his lips refrain from lauding progress and the golden mean. When gas first spread along a city, mapping it forth about evenfall for the eye of observant birds, a new age had begun for sociality and corporate pleasure-seeking. The work of Prometheus had advanced by another stride. Mankind and its supper parties were no longer at the mercy of a few miles of sea-fog; sundown no longer emptied the promenade; and the day was lengthened out to every man's fancy. The city-folk had stars of their own; biddable, domesticated stars.

It is true that these were not so steady, nor yet so clear, as their originals; nor indeed was their lustre so elegant as that of the best wax candles. But then the gas stars, being nearer at hand, were more practically efficacious than Jupiter himself. The lamplighters took to their heels every evening, and ran with a good heart. It was pretty to see man thus emulating the punctuality of heaven's orbs; and though perfection was not absolutely reached, and now and then an individual may have been knocked on the head by the ladder of the flying functionary, people commended his zeal in a proverb – 'God bless the lamplighter!'

God bless him, indeed! For the term of his twilight diligence is near at hand; and for not much longer shall we watch him speeding up the street and, at measured intervals, knocking another luminous hole into the dusk. For another advance has been effected. Our tame stars are to come out in future, not one by one, but all in a body and at once. A sedate electrician somewhere in a back office touches a spring – and behold! from one end to another of the city, from east to west, from the Alexandra to the Crystal Palace, there is light! What a spectacle, on some clear, dark night-fall, from the edge of Hampstead Hill, when in a moment, in the twinkling of an eye, the design of the monstrous city flashes into vision. Star-rise by electricity, the most romantic flight of civilisation; the compensatory benefit for an array of factories and bankers' clerks.

But the conservative, while lauding progress, is ever timid of innovation; his is the hand upheld to counsel pause; his is the signal advising slow advance. The word *electricity* sounds the note of danger. In Paris, at the mouth of the Passage des Princes, in the place before the Opéra portico, and in the Rue Drouot at the Figaro office, a new sort of urban star now shines out nightly, horrible, unearthly, obnoxious to the human eye; a lamp for a nightmare! Such a light as this should shine only on murders and public crime, or along the corridors of lunatic asylums, a horror to heighten horror. To look at it only once is to fall in love with gas, which gives a warm domestic radiance fit to eat by. Mankind might have remained content with what Prometheus stole for them. Yet it is proposed that we should henceforward take our walks abroad in the glare of permanent lighting. A man need not be superstitious if he scruple to follow his pleasures by the light of the Terror that Flieth, nor very epicurean if he prefer to see the face of beauty more becomingly displayed. That ugly blinding glare may not improperly advertise the home of slanderous Figaro, which is a backshop to the infernal regions. But where soft joys prevail, where people are convoked to pleasure and the philosopher looks on staring and silent, where love and laughter, and deifying wine abound, there, at least, let the mild lustre shine upon the ways of man.

From *A Plea for Gas Lamps*, 1881

More Lights

'The evening hour, too, gives us the irresponsibility which darkness and lamplight bestow. We are no longer quite ourselves. As we step out of the house on a fine evening between four and six.'
– Virginia Woolf

'The shops in the buildings that wall in three sides of the square are brilliantly lighted, the air is filled with music and merry voices, and altogether the scene is as bright and spirited and full of cheerfulness as any we could desire. We enjoy it thoroughly.'
– Mark Twain

'This is the brightest and the most animated time. The street lamps rival the stars in number and brilliancy, and if it happens to be moonlight, you can easily read the smallest print; the light has turned blue instead of being yellow, and that is all.'
– Théophile Gautier

'Under Napoleon III the number of gas lanterns increased rapidly. This increased safety in the city made the crowds feel at home in the open streets even at night, and removed the starry sky from the

ambience of the big city more reliably than was done by its tall buildings. "I draw the curtains behind the sun; now it has been put to bed, as is proper; henceforth I shall see no other light." The moon and the stars are no longer worth mentioning.'
– Walter Benjamin

'During his walks Erik Satie was observed stopping to jot down ideas by the light of the streetlamps he passed. During the war, when these lights were often extinguished, a wicked myth circulated that Satie's productivity had dropped as a result.'
– Robert Orledge

'The lights on the waterfront, a long necklace of lamps strung up the mountain-side along the road that passed the bishopric and the occasional red or green of a neon sign – so hideous at close quarters and so pretty from a distance – gave the town the air of a flaunting Babylonian metropolis.'
– Patrick Leigh Fermor

'The lights were cardinal. First there were gaslights, then the silver electricity for which Broadway was re-christened the Great White Way, and finally neon. Now it was the Glittering Gulch, the Fabulous Floodway, the Stem, the Heavenly Hell.'
– Nik Cohn

THÉOPHILE GAUTIER

– Suspicious Lights –

Let me make a call on a friend of my own age; for the young fellows are all on the ramparts, or on the Avron plateau. Happy are the young! Out I go. The night is endowed with a sinister darkness rayed by a slanting, wind-driven rain mingled with flakes of snow. The steam fire-engines on the quays disgorge livid smoke into the obscurity. The Seine runs inky, thick, oily, like the waters of the Styx or the Acheron. In quick succession pass by the river steamers, a light in the bows and another at the stern, their cabin windows streaming with light. They stop at the landing-places, and, in the glare of the lamps and amid a confused swarming of shadows, fantastic and spectral groups become visible. They are wounded men being brought in; at least they will not have to lie on the battlefield until the wan winter morn dawns again, and the cold of night will not bind them with their coagulated blood to the frozen ground. They are carried to the ambulances, where every care awaits them, in carriages and on stretchers. Their glorious day is over, and if pain does not prevent their sleeping, they will dream of victory and deliverance.

On the darkened facade of the Louvre, on the

other side of the river, two windows are blazing so brightly that the red flashes might lead one to suppose the interior on fire. Against the luminous background moving to and fro, like shadow pictures that have not been held close enough to the transparent curtain, are blurred shadows occupied with some serious job. The fire is being blown with a pair of bellows, and as the blaze brightens or fades, the shadows become stronger or fainter. But behind these panes there is not, as would have been taken for granted in the old days of Romanticism, a Ruggieri preparing poisons, or an alchemist looking in his retorts for the philosopher's stone. The cause of that suspicious light is merely a forge, used for the repairing of the rifles of the National Guards.

I cross the Pont des Saints-Pères, and become the sport of the wind, that tries to carry my hat off into the river. In the distance I could feel there were, as in Piranesi's shadowy engravings, opaque architectural masses and lines of quays marked by bright dots like those in blackened cardboard held to the light, but the fiery pearls were scattered far apart and no longer formed that brilliant line of light which forms the customary illumination of Paris.

The impression the scene made on me was one of sadness, solemnity, and grandeur. Through the broad arches guarded by the colossal statues of Peace and War, the Place du Carrousel showed shimmering with water, glaced with reflections and crossed by a single bus, the red lights of which glared like the eyes of some monstrous insect crawling through the darkness.

After traversing a number of streets, that were so dark they looked exactly like saw-cuts in blocks of black marble, I reached my friend's house, and found he had fared forth in search of news, this being the food still sought for most eagerly, poor as may be one's meals. I had perforce to return home, and once back, my feet in front of a widow's fire, by the light of a single wax candle, for in times of siege one must economise both fire and lights, and in my hand a book taken at random from the deal board on which rest the few volumes saved from my library, I began sadly enough my solitary evening.

From 'Paris Besieged',
The Works of Théophile Gautier, 1902

JEAN-PAUL CLÉBERT

– With Ectoplasmic Ease –

There is an alarming number of dingbats wandering about in the moonlight. Not mean or screaming lunatics, slavering and glaring murderously, but frighteningly thin human beings walking in silence, flitting past, so to speak, about two or three centimetres above the asphalt, hands in pockets, collar pulled up in the midsummer heat, forelock wild, eyes unfocussed, passing down the street, by houses and people, and through the city with ectoplasmic ease, pausing only to observe a cat, or the kids at play in the squares, asking for food neither at shelter doors nor of their peers ensconced on benches, and never, ever, entering a bistro. One or two have musical instruments under their arm.

From *Paris Vagabond*,
translated by Donald Nicholson-Smith, 2016

THOMAS DE QUINCEY

– Saturday Nights –

I always feel on a Saturday night, as though I were released from some yoke of labour, had some wages to receive, and some luxury of repose to enjoy. On these nights, after taking opium, I used often to wander the streets, without much regard to the direction or the distance, to all the markets and other parts of the city to which the poor resort on this night, for laying out their wages. Many a family party, consisting of a man, his wife, and sometimes one or two of his children, have I listened to, as they passed me by consulting on their ways and means, or the strength of their exchequer, or the price of household articles. Gradually I became familiar with their wishes, their difficulties, and their opinions. Sometimes there might be heard murmurs of discontent; but far oftener expressions on the countenance, or words uttered in patience, hope, and tranquillity. Whenever I saw occasion, or could do it without appearing to be intrusive, I joined their parties; and gave my opinion upon the matters in hand, which, if not always judicious, were always received indulgently. If wages were a little higher, or expected to be so, or the quartern loaf a little lower, or if it was reported that onions and butter were expected to fall, I was glad. Yet, if the contrary were true, I drew from the opium some means of consoling myself. For opium (like the bee, that extracts its materials indiscriminately from roses and from the soot of chimneys) can overrule all feelings into a compliance with the master key.

Some of these Saturday rambles led me to great distances: for an opium-eater is too happy to observe the motion of time. And sometimes in my attempts to steer homewards, upon nautical principles, by fixing my eye on the pole-star, and seeking ambitiously for a northwest passage, instead of circumnavigating all the capes and headlands I had doubled in my outward voyage, I came suddenly upon such knotty problems as alleyways, such enigmatical entries, and such sphinx's riddles as streets without thoroughfares – as must baffle the audacity of porters and confound the intellects of hackney-coachmen. I could almost have believed, at times, that I might be the first discoverer of some of these terra incognita, and doubted whether they had ever been laid down in the modern charts of the city.

From *Confessions of an English Opium-Eater*, 1821

JOHN BURROUGHS

– Sunday Night –

At Chester I stopped overnight, and selected my hotel for its name, the 'Green Dragon'. It was Sunday night, and the only scene my rambles presented to me was quite a large gathering of persons on a corner, listening, with apparent indifference or curiosity, to a hot-headed preacher in the thickening dark – 'Now I am going to tell you something you will not like to hear . . . something that will make you angry. I know it will. It is this. I expect to go to heaven. I am perfectly confident I shall go there. And I know you do not like that!' But why his hearers should not like that did not appear. For my part, I thought, for the good of all concerned, the sooner he moved on the better.

From *The Writings of John Burroughs*, 1904

RAINER MARIA RILKE

– Midnight Mass? –

I thought there would perhaps be midnight Mass and went out after eleven; the streets and footpaths between the walls lay there long, like lowered outspread banners, black and white, made of a strip of wall shadow beside a strip of light; for it was the first night after full moon, and the moon stood very high in the sky and sharply outshone all the stars, so that only here and there a distant big one flared so strongly that some darkness was formed about it. How the illumined rims of the walls dazzled, how the leaves of the olives were made entirely of night, as if cut out of skies, old, no longer used night skies. And the mountain slopes had such an air of lunar decay and towered up out of the houses like something unmastered. And the houses were dark, and where the wooden shutters had not been closed over them, the windows had the faded, translucent look of blind eyes. Finally, on the little piazza under the clock tower, there was standing a crowd of Capri youths in rendezvous. Out of a little coffeehouse with red curtains, which was set into the blackest corner, came now and then the impatient rattling of a tambourine . . . A step in wooden shoes clattered along by the houses, the clock began and struck the last quarter before midnight. But the church was shut, as if it had been shut for decades. And what rang out from over there, far off and oddly penetrating, from the olive slopes and from the vineyards, was no Christian singing. Heavy voices full of old wavering laments, long drawn out, without beginning, not as if they were suddenly starting – only as if one's ear were unexpectedly tuned to some continuously held tone; voices seemingly fetched out again from the hearing of remote mountain-faces; voices that come into being of themselves, as though the night wind were caught in the soul of an animal; long, heavy, wavering voices, calls and series of calls of a primeval natural drunkenness, dull, unconscious, more tolerated than willed, and intermittently, laughter breaking out flamelike and quickly consuming itself, short, alert, and warm as out of a summer night, and then again, moonlight; paths, walls, houses, an earth of moonlight, of moon shadow, that keeps still while with strange meaningfulness New Year's midnight strikes, slowly laying stroke on stroke: each all smooth, all spread out, foldless, as if it were to be preserved like that.

I had gone back again to my little house and stood up on its roof and wanted to see a good end in all that . . .

From *Letter to Clara Rilke*, 1907, translated by
Jane Bannard Greene and M. D. Herter Norton, 1945

CHARLES DICKENS

– At Half-Past Twelve –

Some years ago, a temporary inability to sleep, referable to a distressing impression, caused me to walk about the streets all night, for a series of several nights. The disorder might have taken a long time to conquer, if it had been faintly experimented on in bed; but, it was soon defeated by the brisk treatment of getting up directly after lying down, and going out, and coming home tired at sunrise. In the course of those nights, I finished my education in a fair amateur experience of houselessness. My principal object being to get through the night, the pursuit of it brought me into sympathetic relations with people who have no other object every night in the year. The month was March, and the weather damp, cloudy, and cold. The sun not rising before half-past five, the night perspective looked sufficiently long at half-past twelve: which was about my time for confronting it. The restlessness of a great city, and the way in which it tumbles and tosses before it can get to sleep, formed one of the first entertainments offered to the contemplation of us houseless people. It lasted about two hours. We lost a great deal of companionship when the late public-houses turned their lamps out, and when the policemen thrust the last brawling drunkards into the street; but stray vehicles and stray people were left us, after that. If we were very lucky, a policeman's rattle sprang and a fray turned up; but, in general, surprisingly little of this diversion was provided. Except in the Haymarket, which is the worst kept part of London, and about Kent-street in the Borough, and along a portion of the line of the Old Kent-road, the peace was seldom violently broken. But, it was always the case that London, as if in imitation of individual citizens belonging to it, had expiring fits and starts of restlessness. After all seemed quiet, if one cab rattled by, half a dozen would surely follow; and houselessness even observed that intoxicated people appeared to be magnetically attracted towards each other: so that we knew when we saw one drunken object staggering against the shutters of a shop, that another drunken object would stagger up before five minutes were out, to fraternise or fight with it. When we made a divergence from the regular species of drunkard, the thin-armed puff-faced leaden-lipped gin-drinker, and encountered a rarer specimen of a more decent appearance, fifty to one but that specimen was dressed in soiled mourning. As the street experience in the night, so the street experience in the day; the common folk who come unexpectedly into a little property, come unexpectedly into a deal of liquor. At length these flickering sparks would die away, worn out – the last veritable sparks of waking life trailed from some late pie-man or hot potato man – and London would sink to rest. And then the yearning of the houseless mind would be for any sign of company, any lighted place, any movement, anything suggestive of any one being up – nay, even so much as awake, for the houseless eye looked out for lights in windows.

Walking the streets under the pattering rain, houselessness would walk and walk and walk, seeing nothing but the interminable tangle of streets, save at a corner, here and there, two policemen in conversation, or the sergeant or inspector looking after his men. Now and then in the night – but rarely – houselessness would become aware of a furtive head peering out of a doorway a few yards before him, and, coming up with the head, would find a man standing bolt upright to keep within the doorway's shadow, and evidently intent upon no particular service to society. Under a kind of fascination, and in a ghostly silence suitable to the time, Houselessness and this gentleman would eye one another from head to foot, and so, without exchange of speech, part, mutually suspicious. Drip, drip, drip, from ledge and coping, splash from pipes and waterspouts, and by-and-by the houseless shadow would fall upon the stones that pave the way to Waterloo-bridge; it being in the houseless mind to have a halfpennyworth of excuse for saying 'Good night' to the toll-keeper, and catching a glimpse of his fire. A good fire and a good great-coat and a good woollen neck-shawl, were comfortable things to see in conjunction with the toll-keeper; also his brisk wakefulness was excellent company when he rattled the change of halfpence down upon that metal table of his, like a man who defied the night, with all its sorrowful thoughts. There was need of encouragement on the threshold of the bridge, for the bridge was dreary. The chopped up murdered man had not been lowered with a rope over the parapet when those nights were; he was alive, and slept then quietly enough most likely, and undisturbed by any dream of where he was to come. But the river had an awful look, the buildings on the banks were muffled in black shrouds, and the reflected lights seemed to originate deep in the water, as if the spectres of suicides were holding them to show where they went down. The wild moon and clouds were as restless as an evil conscience in a tumbled bed, and the very shadow of the immensity of London seemed to lie oppressively upon the river.

From 'Night Walks', in *The Uncommercial Traveller*, 1861

LEIGH HUNT

– At One –

The readers of these our lucubrations need not be informed that we keep no carriage. The consequence is, that being visitors of the theatre, and having some inconsiderate friends who grow pleasanter and pleasanter till one in the morning, we are great walkers home by night; and this has made us acquaintances of watchmen, moonlight, mud-light, and other accompaniments of that interesting hour.

Luckily we are fond of a walk by night. It does not always do us good; but that is not the fault of the hour, but our own, who ought to be stouter; and therefore we extract what good we can get out of our necessity with becoming temper.

We confess there are points liable to cavil in a walk home by night in February. Old umbrellas have their weak sides; and the quantity of mud and rain may surmount the picturesque. Mistaking a soft piece of mud for hard mud, and so filling your shoe with it, especially at setting out, must be acknowledged as 'aggravating'. But then you ought to have boots. There are sights, indeed, in the streets of London, which can be rendered pleasant by no philosophy; but we must premise that our walk leads us out of town, and through streets and suburbs of by no means the worst description. Even there, we may be grieved if we will.

The farther the walk into the country, the more tiresome we may choose to find it; and when we take it purely to oblige others, we must allow, as in the case of a friend of ours, that generosity itself on two legs may find limits to the notion of virtue being its own reward, and reasonably 'curse those comfortable people' who, by the lights in their windows, are getting into their warm beds, and saying to one another: 'Bad thing to be out of doors to-night.'

Supposing, then, that we are in a reasonable state of health and comfort in other respects, we say that a walk home at night has its merits, if you choose to meet with them. The worst part of it is the setting out; the closing of the door upon the kind faces that part with you. But their words and looks, on the other hand, may set you off well. We have known a word last us all the way home, and a look make a dream of it. To a lover, for instance, no walk can be bad. He sees but one face in the rain and darkness; the same that he saw by the light in the warm room. This ever accompanies him, looking into his eyes; and if the most pitiable and spoilt face in the world should come between them, startling him with the saddest mockery of love, he would treat it kindly for her sake. But this is abegging of the question. A lover does not walk. He is sensible neither to the pleasures nor to the pains of walking. He treads on air; and in the thick of all that appears inclement has an avenue of light and velvet spread for him, like a sovereign prince.

To resume, then, like men of this world. The advantage of a late hour is that everything is silent and the people fast in their beds. This gives the whole world a tranquil appearance. Inanimate objects are no calmer than passions and cares now seem to be all laid asleep. The human being is motionless as the house or the tree; sorrow is suspended; and you endeavour to think that only love is awake. Let not readers of true delicacy be alarmed, for we mean to touch profanely upon nothing that ought to be sacred; and as we are only thinking the best on these occasions, it is of the best love we think; love of no heartless order, and such that ought to be awake with the stars.

By this time the hackney-coaches have all left the stands – a good symptom of their having got their day's money. Crickets are heard, here and there, amidst the embers of some kitchen. A dog follows us. Will nothing make him 'go along'? We dodge him in vain; we run; we stand and 'hish!' at him, accompanying the prohibition with dehortatory gestures, and an imaginary picking up of a stone. We turn again, and there he is vexing our skirts. He even forces us into an angry doubt about whether he will not starve, if we do not let him go home with us. Now if we could but lame him without being cruel; or if we were only an overseer, or a beadle, or a dealer in dog-skin; or a political economist, to think dogs unnecessary. Oh come, he has turned a corner, he has gone; we think we see him trotting off at a distance, thin and muddy, and our heart misgives us. But it was not our fault; we were not 'hishing' at the time. His departure was lucky, for he had got our enjoyments into a dilemma. We resume our way, independent and alone; for we have no companion this time. A fellow-pedestrian is company – is the party you have left; you talk and laugh, and there is no longer anything to be contended with. But alone, and in bad weather, and with a long way to go, here is something for the temper and spirits to grapple with and turn to account; and accordingly we are booted and buttoned up, an umbrella over our heads, the rain pelting upon it, and the lamp-light shining in the gutters. 'Mud-shine', as an artist of our acquaintance used to call it, with a gusto of reprobation. There is a pleasure in overcoming obstacles; mere action is something; imagination is more; and the spinning of the blood, and vivacity of the mental endeavour, act well upon one another, and gradually put you in a state of robust consciousness and triumph. Every time you set your leg down you have respect for it. The umbrella is held in the hand like a roaring trophy.

We are now reaching the country. The fog and rain are over and we meet our old friends – the watchmen. Staid, heavy, indifferent, more coat than man, pondering, yet not pondering, old but not reverend, immensely useless. No; useless they are not; for the inmates of the houses think them otherwise, and in that imagination they do good. We do not pity the watchmen as we used to. Old age often cares little for regular sleep. They would not be sleeping, perhaps, if they were in their beds; and certainly they would not be earning. What sleep they get is perhaps sweeter in the watch-box – a forbidden sweet – and they have a sense of importance, and a claim on the persons in-doors, which, together with the amplitude of their coating, and the possession of the box itself, make them feel themselves, not without reason, to be 'somebody'. They are peculiar and official.

Yet characters are to be found among watchmen. They are not all mere coat, and lump, and indifference. By-the-way, what do they think of in general? How do they vary the monotony of their ruminations from one to two, and from two to three, and so on?

Of characters, or rather varieties among watchmen, we remember several. One was a Dandy Watchman, who used to ply at the top of Oxford Street, next to the park. We called him the dandy, on account of his utterance. He had a mincing way with it, pronouncing the 'a' in the word 'past' as it is in 'hat' making a little preparatory 'hem' before he spoke, and then bringing out his 'past ten' in a style of genteel indifference; as if, upon the whole, he was of that opinion.

Another was the Metallic Watchman, who paced the same street towards Hanover Square, and had a clang in his voice like a trumpet. He was a voice and nothing else; but any difference is something in a watchman.

A third, who cried the hour in Bedford Square, was remarkable in his calling for being abrupt and loud. There was a fashion among his tribe at that time of omitting the words 'past' and 'o'clock', and crying only the number of the hour. I know not whether a recollection I have of his performance one night is entire fact, or whether some fancies of what might have taken place are mixed up with it – but my impression is, that as I was turning the corner into the square with a friend, and was in the midst of a discussion in which numbers were concerned, we were suddenly startled, as if in solution of it, by a brief and tremendous outcry of – ONE!

A fourth watchman was a very singular phenomenon: Reading Watchman. He had a book, which he read by the light of his lantern. It seemed cruel to pitch amidst so many discomforts and privations one who had imagination enough to wish to be relieved from them. Nothing but a sluggish vacuity befits a watchman.

But the oddest of all was the Sliding Watchman. Think of walking up a street in the depth of a frosty winter, with long ice in the gutters, and sleet overhead, and then figure to yourself a sort of bale of a man in white coming sliding towards you with a lantern in one hand, and an umbrella over his head. It was the oddest mixture of luxury and hardship, of juvenility and old age! But this looked agreeable. Animal spirits carry everything before them; and our invincible friend seemed a watchman for Rabelais. Time was run at and butted by him, like a goat. The slide seemed to bear him half through the night at once. He slipped from out of his box and at one rush of a merry thought, seemed to say, 'Everything's in imagination – here goes the whole weight of my office.'

But we approach our home. How still the trees! How deliciously asleep the country! How beautifully grim and nocturnal this wooded avenue of ascent against the cold white sky! The watchmen and patrols, which the careful citizens have planted in abundance within a mile of their doors, salute us – and not so welcome as we pretend; for we ought not to be out so late; and it is one of the assumptions of these fatherly old fellows to remind us of it. Some fowls, who have made a strange roost in a tree, flutter as we pass them. Another pull up the hill, unyielding; a few strides on a level; and there is the light in the window, the eye of the warm soul of the house – one's home again. How particular, and yet how universal, is that word; and how surely does it deposit everyone for himself in his own nest!

From 'Walks Home by Night', *Watchmen*, 1828

LOGAN PEARSALL SMITH

– The Word –

I thanked the club porter who helped me into my coat, and stepped out lightly into the vastness and freshness of the Night. And as I walked along my eyes were dazzling with the glare I had left; I still seemed to hear the sound of my speech, and the applause and laughter.

And when I looked up at the Stars, the great Stars that bore me company, streaming over the dark houses as I moved, I felt that I was the Lord of Life; the mystery and disquieting meaninglessness of existence – the existence of other people, and of my own, were solved for me now. As for the Earth, hurrying beneath my feet, how bright was its journey; how shining the goal towards which it went swinging – you might really say leaping – through the sky.

'I must tell the Human Race of this!' I heard my voice; saw my prophetic gestures, as I expounded the ultimate meaning of existence to the white, rapt faces of Humanity. Only to find the words – that troubled me; were there then no words to describe this Vision – divine – intoxicating?

And then *the* Word struck me. The Word people would use. I stopped in the street; my Soul was silenced like a bell that snarls at a jarring touch. I stood there awhile and meditated on language, its perfidious meanness, the inadequacy, the ignominy of our vocabulary, and how Moralists have spoiled our words by distilling into them, as into little vials of poison, all their hatred of human joy. Away with that police-force of brutal words which bursts in on our best moments and arrests our finest feelings! This music within me, large, like the song of the stars – like a Glory of Angels singing . . .

'No one has any right to say I am drunk!' I shouted.

From *Trivia,* 1917

KATE PULLINGER

– Walk Number One, or Walk Number Two? –

When I walk alone at night I like to dream, as though I am asleep in bed already. I dream about where I've been, and what I'll tell people about where I've been, who said what, and why, and what it was like to listen to them. Why did they say that? Wasn't that funny?! I walk in my own warm fug and, before I know it, benevolence creeps up on me, and I'm in love with the city, in love with the world, all over again.

At night I have two routes home to choose from: if I get off at this stop there are people and buses and cars and bikes and children – always children, no matter how late.

If I get off at the other stop, the streets are empty. The streetlamps flicker, the cars woosh by, and every corner is darker than the last.

Not a lot to choose between, these two routes, you might think. Think again: Walk Number One, with its bright lights and big people, takes well over 15 minutes. Walk Number Two takes 10 minutes, less, in fact, because I make myself walk so quickly. If I go the dark way, which I do more often than not, I know myself to be lazy and brave and foolhardy, an uneasy, unrewarding, combination.

It's a girl thing, I guess, a woman's lot, being nervous when walking alone at night. We are told to be afraid, so we are. I thought I was above all that: I don't believe that the city is more dangerous than the country. When I take Walk Number One I'm bold and brassy and happy; and yet, when I take Walk Number Two it's a different story. When I set out I'm jumpy, I'm nervy, every lone male is a threat. I scuttle along looking forwards, backwards, sideways, clutching my phone and my bag and my keys, my hat pulled down, my scarf wound tight, my coat zipped up to the top, gloved and booted as though my outerwear will protect me from whatever comes my way. Click click click go my heels on the pavement, whump whump whump goes my bag against my hip, boom boom boom goes my paranoia.

The shorter route, the one I somehow always end up taking, passes through a low-rise council estate where all the curtains are shut and no one stirs no matter what time of day, like the night of the living dead where even the living dead have died. Then I walk past the entrance to a football stadium. Sometimes the road is crowded with supporters on their way to or from a match; but mostly the stadium just sits there, like the huge shell of an extinct species of turtle, a reminder of better days.

If I went the other way, the other route that takes a bit longer, the friendly route that I could take if I wasn't, let face it, more lazy than I am afraid, this is what I would find – food. A lot of it. West Indian roti, Lebanese pastries, Thai noodles, Greek vine leaves, Syrian barbecue, Polish dumplings, English fish and chips, fried chicken that comes from just about anywhere except Kentucky. If I went this way, I could eat my way home; at night on this street everything stays open way past my bedtime. These eating places teem with humanity, people out with their friends, entire families with countless children, the multiplicity of migrants and natives who travel through this city. I should always choose this route: there is no choice, really.

But I hardly ever go this way. As the train clatters along on its rails I get to this stop and I think, if I get off here it will take me fifteen minutes, and if I get off at the next stop it will take me ten minutes, and I'm a little tired, and yes, I'm a little lazy. And so I stay on the train and it shudders along the rails and I get off at the next stop and my first thought is, oh, oh yeah, I forgot, this way is scary. It's dark, and windswept, and empty, like an urban cliché from a British gangster movie.

And yet, to tell you the truth, nothing has ever happened to me when I walk this walk at night. Nothing. Back on Walk Number One, the walk I prefer though, turns out, I hardly ever go that way, stuff happens all the time. Someone tried to blow up a train at my stop not too long ago. He failed in his mission but it's the thought that counts. Closer to my place, there was a shoot-out in one of the fried chicken cafes. It was winter, and dark and I was herding a great crowd of children along the street that night – my two, and their friends who, when you are out in the streets with them, seem to divide and multiply like human clones, until you've got god knows how many flapping around your legs. The children, being children, were busy discussing the Philosophy of Five-Year-Olds and other august topics and didn't notice a thing. Not even the car sticking out of the estate agent's window. And there also was a police cordon. Sounds dramatic, but it wasn't really. We made our way home quite happily, the children oblivious, as always.

But most of the time, nothing happens. I weigh it up in my idle way – fifteen minutes or ten, ten or fifteen? I get off at the second stop and I hoik my bag onto my shoulder, pull on my gloves, push down my hat, and I walk. I like to watch the lights – car headlamps, the streetlights overhead, the neon and fluorescence and sodium – the way the lights spread out and sparkle in the cool night air, fragmented by the rain or made harder and brighter by a clear night sky. They tell women to be aware on night walks, to be aware of who is in front of you, who is behind you, to be alert, whichever route you choose to take. But eventually, I forget about that. The rhythm of walking lulls me like a tide.

And I turn into my street. There's my front door, white, with yellow light leaking out from the internal hallway. When my kids were babies and my nights out felt rare, I'd pause outside the door, to prepare myself for going inside, to enjoy my last moments alone night-walking, to stay inside my head a minute or two longer. Then I go in, and shut the door, and leave the night, and the city, and the walking behind.

From *The Essay: Nightwalks*, BBC Radio, 2007

THOMAS CORYAT

– Braves –

There are certaine desperate and resolute villaines called Braves, who at some unlawfull times do commit great villainy. They wander abroad very late in the night to and fro for their prey, like hungry Lyons, being armed with a privy coate of maile, a gauntlet upon their right hand, and a little sharpe dagger called a stiletto. They lurke commonly by the water side, and if at their time of the night, which is betwixt eleven of the clocke and two, they happen to meete any man walking along that is worth the rifling, they will presently stabbe him, take away all about him that is of any worth, and when they have throughly pulled his plumes, they will throw him into one of the channels. But they buy this booty very deare if they are afterwards apprehended. For they are presently executed.

From *Coryat's Crudities Hastily Gobled Up in Five Moneths Travels*, 1611

– Road Kids and Stiffs, and Bindle-Stiffs –

Road-kids are nice little chaps – when you get them alone and they are telling you 'how it happened'. But take my word for it, watch out for them when they roam in a pack. Then they are wolves, and like wolves they are capable of dragging down the strongest man. At such times they are not cowardly. They will fling themselves upon a man and hold on with every ounce of strength in their wiry bodies, till he is thrown and helpless.

Drunken men are the especial prey of the road-kids. Robbing a drunken man they call 'rolling a stiff'; and wherever they are, they are on the constant lookout for drunks. The drunk is their particular meat, as the fly is the particular meat of the spider. The rolling of a stiff is oft-times an amusing sight, especially when the stiff is helpless and when interference is unlikely. More than once have I seen them do it, and I know whereof I speak.

A vision comes to me. It is a dark night. My push is along the sidewalk in the suburbs. Ahead of us, under an electric light, a man crosses the street diagonally. There is something tentative and desultory in his walk. The kids scent the game on the instant. The man is drunk. He blunders across the opposite sidewalk and is lost in the darkness as he takes a short-cut through a vacant lot. No hunting cry is raised, but the pack flings itself forward in quick pursuit. In the middle of the vacant lot it comes upon him. But what is this? – snarling and strange forms, small and dim and menacing, are between the pack and its prey. It is another pack of road-kids, and in the hostile pause we learn that it is their meat, that they have been trailing it a dozen blocks and more and that we are butting in. But it is the world primeval. These wolves are baby wolves. (As a matter of fact, I don't think one of them was over twelve or thirteen years of age. I met some of them afterward, and learned that they had just arrived that day over the hill, and that they hailed from Denver and Salt Lake City.) Our pack flings forward. The baby wolves squeal and screech and fight like little demons. All about the drunken man rages the struggle for the possession of him. Down he goes in the thick of it, and the combat rages over his body after the fashion of the Greeks and Trojans over the body and armor of a fallen hero. Amid cries and tears and wailings the baby wolves are dispossessed, and my pack rolls the stiff.

But always I remember the poor stiff and his befuddled amazement at the abrupt eruption of battle in the vacant lot. I see him now, dim in the darkness, titubating in stupid wonder, good naturedly essaying the role of peacemaker in that multitudinous scrap the significance of which he did not understand, and the really hurt expression on his face when he, unoffending he, was clutched at by many hands and dragged down in the thick of the press.

'Bindle-stiffs' are also favorite prey of the road-kids. A bindle-stiff is a working tramp. He takes his name from the roll of blankets he carries on his travels, which is known as a 'bindle'. Because he does work, a bindle-stiff is expected to have some small change about him, and it is after that small change that the road-kids go. The best hunting-ground for bindle-stiffs is in the sheds and barns on the edges of a city, and the time for tracking and hunting is the night, when the bindle-stiff seeks these places to roll up in his blankets and sleep.

From *The Road*, 1907

JOHN BROWN

– I Travelled by Night, that Being the Safe Time –

I laid in a stock of corn-bread, and having obtained a forged pass from a poor white man, for which I gave him an old hen, I stole off one night, about two months after I had procured the pass, and made for the high road, which I thought would lead me straight to England. I walked all night, and when dawn came hid myself in the wood, starting again when it began to get dusk. I went this way a great many nights, keeping to the main road, and concealing myself by day in the woods or swamps. My only direction was to take the biggest road. One night I came to one, which, after I had followed it for some time – still under the impression that it would take me to England – brought me to a dead stop, at a stone quarry, at the foot of the Blue Ridge of mountains. I stayed here all night, walking about to keep clear of the wild cats and panthers, which I could hear prowling about, and whose growling alarmed me very much. When dawn broke I began to consider what I should do.

*

I started on my travels once more. I watched until

the negro quarters had been inspected, then skulked out into the yard, where I had observed a small skiff. I dragged it down to the water, and crossed over to the Arkansas side, the river here being about a mile in width. Having reached the bank, I turned the skiff adrift. I had chosen this mode of making my escape, because I knew the skiff would be missed, and they would conclude I had gone towards New Orleans, and would hunt for me in that direction, never suspecting I should strike up stream. I think I was right in this conjecture. Anyhow, here I was safe for the present, and I set off walking as hard as I could put my foot to the ground.

*

During my journey I observed the plan I had followed on former occasions; namely, walking by night, and lying by for rest and concealment in the day, sleeping behind logs, like a wild man. I guided my course by following the muddy waters of the Mississippi, but I was frequently baulked by coming to inlets or bayous. These are much lower than the bed of the river, and are full of alligators. I used to hear these creatures at night, snorting and plashing about in the water – to my mortal terror – as I did not know that, at any moment, I might fall into their hungry jaws! When I came to one of these bayous I would follow the bank until I encountered a ferry. Here I would stop, and watching for an opportunity, would draw the staple that kept the boat fastened, then cross over in the boat to the opposite side, where I would leave it. I would then go down that bank until I reached the Mississippi again. I lived, or rather sustained life, by eating raw corn, potatoes, pine roots, and sassafras buds. The country I passed through appeared to be thinly inhabited; there was, however, plenty of wood and reed cane, so I found no difficulty in hiding myself, even near to the water's edge. From these places of concealment I used to watch the steamers going up and down the river; and these served to guide me on my course, for I knew they must start from somewhere, and I hoped that I might find friends there, and rest for a time. Moving on, I at last reached a great town where the steamers were in large numbers. I cannot say how long I was getting to it; many weary days and nights I do know. I judge it must have taken me at least three months.

*

It was thirty miles from a friend's house, and he impressed upon me the necessity of making up my mind to accomplish the distance before day-break, or I should certainly be lost; that is, captured. Of course, with such a prospect before me, I had every inducement to task my remaining strength to the utmost, to cover the ground within the time. Though it was now the month of August, and the space between nightfall and daybreak was short for me to do what was before me. As soon as dusk fell, I set out with a stout heart.

What I endured that dense night will never be effaced from my memory. I had received general instructions for guidance on the road, and been told which villages I should go through. But in order to avoid incurring unnecessary risk, when I reached a village, instead of passing through it, I would make a turn and go round it, endeavouring to strike the road a little beyond. This did not always succeed. More than once, after going right round one side of a village, and coming to a road, my heart misgave me, and in obedience to a presentiment that all was not right, I turned back, and beat on until I struck another road, even retracing my steps more than once, until I came to the road that left no misgiving in my mind, and I would go on again into the dark – as brave as a lion!

Many people will say I was superstitious. And I was. But the feeling was an instinct, whose cautions, even in the present day, I cannot help minding.

In this way I walked the whole night. As dawn came I had the satisfaction of seeing from far off, the town I was making for, and soon after, I enjoyed the still greater pleasure of finding myself in a place of safety.

From *Slave Life in Georgia*, 1855

FANNY KEMBLE

– My Father Proposed a Walk –

My father proposed a walk, and we sallied forth. We walked to the end of Broadway, a distance of two miles, I should think, and then back again. The moon was lighting the whole upper sky, but every now and then, as we crossed the streets that led to the river, we caught glimpses of the water, and woody banks, and the sky that hung over them, that I never saw but in Claude's pictures. After walking nearly a mile up Broadway, we came to Canal Street: it is broader and finer than any I have seen in New York; and at one end of it, a Christian church, copied from some Pagan temple or other, looked exceedingly well, in the full flood of silver light that streamed from heaven. There were many temptations to look around, but the flags were so horribly broken and out of order, that to do so was to run the risk of breaking one's neck. The street was very much thronged, and I thought the crowd a more civil and orderly one than an English crowd. The men did not jostle or push one another, or tread upon one's feet, or kick down one's shoe heels, or crush one's bonnet into one's face, or turn it round upon one's head, all which I have seen done in London streets. There is this to be said: the crowd was abroad merely for pleasure, sauntering along, which is a thing never seen in London; the proportion of idle loungers who frequent these streets being very inconsiderable, when compared with the number of people going on business through the town. I observed that the young men tonight made room for women to pass, and many of them, as they drew near us, took the cigar from their mouth, which I thought especially courteous. They were all smoking, to a man, except those who were spitting, which helped to remind me of Paris, to which the whole place bore a slight resemblance. The shops appear to make no show whatever, and will not bear a comparison with the brilliant display of the Parisian boulevards or the rich magnificence of our own, in that respect. The women dress very much, and very much like French women gone mad. All of them seem to me to walk horribly ill, as if they wore tight shoes. Came in rather tired, took tea, sang an immensity, wrote journal, and looked at the peerless moon.

*

After dinner, sat writing my journal till ten, when father returned. The moon was shining soft and full, and he asked me if I would take a walk. I bonneted and booted, and we sallied forth. The moon withdrew behind a veil of thin white clouds, but left a grey clear light over the earth, and through the sky. We reached the Fair Mount bridge at about eleven.

The turnpike was fast, and everybody asleep, so we climbed over the gate, and very deliberately pursued our way over the strange dark-looking covered bridge. The glimmering lamps, at distant intervals, threw crossing beams and rafters into momentary brightness, that had a strange effect contrasted with the surrounding gloom. We reached the other side, and, turning off from the road, began climbing the hill opposite the breakwater. The road was muddy in the valley with heavy rains; and unwilling to wade through the dirt, we clambered along a paling for several yards, and so escaped the mire. My father steered for the grassy knoll just opposite Fair Mount; and there, screened by a thicket of young cedar bushes, with the river breaking over the broad dam below, and the shadowy banks on the other side melting away in the soft grey light, we sat down on a tree trunk. Here we remained for a quarter of an hour without uttering a syllable; indeed, we had not spoken three words since we set out. My father was thinking, I presume, of something. We were disturbed by a large white spaniel dog, who, coming down from among the cedar bushes, reminded me of the old witch stories, and Faust. We arose to depart, and took our way towards the Market Street bridge, along the banks of the river. The broken notes of a bugle-horn came at intervals across the sleeping waters from the opposite shore, where there reflected the few lingering lights from the houses that had not yet shut up for the night. The moon, faintly struggling through the clouds, touched the dark pyramids of the cedar trees that rose into the grey sky, and threw our shadows on the lonely path we were pursuing. It cast a pale gleam through the rapid clouds that chased one another like dreams across the sky. The air was as soft and balmy as the night air of August. The world was still; and excepting our footfalls as we trudged along, no sound disturbed the universal repose. We did not reach home till half-past twelve. We walked down Market Street, through the long ranges of casks. We were the only creatures stirring, excepting some melancholy night-loving cat. Now my father said calmly, 'How I do wish I had a gimlet.' – 'What for?'– 'What fun it would be to pierce every one of these barrels.' For a gentleman of his years, this appeared to me rather a juvenile prompting of Satan; and as I laughingly expostulated on the wickedness of such a proceeding, he replied with much innocence, 'I don't think they'd ever suspect me of having done it;' – and truly I don't think they would. Came home, and to bed. That was a curious fancy of my father's.

From *Journal of a Residence in America*, 1835

ETHEL LYNN

– Night Cap –

As we rose to say good-night and head off, Mrs Adams produced milk, eggs and whiskey, and they both prepared a customary night cap. I was startled by the enormous draught of liquor poured out by Mr Adams who, noting my surprise, remarked apologetically, 'I've been a frightful sufferer from insomnia for a number of years. That was one of the reasons which led me to adopt this mode of living, but even the open air has failed to relieve me. I've tried everything, vigorous exercise, and nightly walks, and I've found my only relief in these stiff jolts of whiskey. At times I am compelled to get up in the night and find the bottle. But I never become intoxicated.'

'I should think that sort of thing would ruin your digestion.'

'Well, I take certain precautions. I always take my evening dram in the form of an eggnog, and if I need a drink in the night, I take a large cup of milk first, which seems to prevent any untoward effects.'

From *The Adventures of a Woman Hobo*, 1917

ANNABEL ABBS

– Discombobulated Journey –

I buy some bread, lettuce and cheese, then decide to check Google Maps for the quickest way back to my room. When I take out my phone it's dead but I'm fairly sure I can find my way, in spite of the darkness and the gusting snow. I walk fast, fearful in these unlit, unpeopled streets. All the houses are the same in Santa Fe – city policy apparently – and I become disorientated. After twenty minutes I'm utterly lost. I appear to be outside the city, on the edge of a vast, black highway. Trucks and cars spin past me, their red tail lights disappearing into an ocean of darkness. The pavement tapers perilously to a kerb the width of my foot. I take a side road that feels to be in the right direction. The snow is melting into my jeans, settling into the creases of my coat and I just want to get back to my warm little room with its crooked lamp, its cheerful cushions, its miniature kettle. The road is lined on one side with trees, which doesn't feel right. Surely if I were heading towards the city, there would be more concrete and fewer trees?

The emptiness of this side road frightens me – not only are there no pedestrians or street lights, there are no passing cars, no houses. No lights of any sort. Tears prickle at my eyes. I'm lost and cold, without a working phone, without anyone to ask. I start running back down the highway, but I kept stumbling and tripping because the unrepaired pavements undulate and veer – they're designed for trucks emerging from parking lots rather than for walkers. Suddenly I'm running and tumbling and sobbing all at once. In my mania I walk into a vast plastic garbage bin and send it rattling down the road.

When I get back to the huge black highway, I notice a man ahead of me. He's the first pedestrian I've clocked in an hour of frantic, discombobulated walking. I'm so startled I stop sobbing and run towards him in a great rush of relief. 'Excuse me, where's Santa Fe?' I gasp. He looks at me wide-eyed, as stunned to see another walker as I am. Or perhaps he's only stunned by the red-eyed wildness of my appearance. He points up the road and says if I walk for half an hour I'll reach the city.

I start the trek back, slaloming between huge plastic bins and cursing the endlessly buckling pavement, the snow, the inky sky, myself for having such a hopeless sense of direction. Most of all I curse America for its callous disregard for pavements and its monotonous, unbending miles of motorway.

At the next corner I see the neon flash of a drive-thru McDonald's and the lights of Santa Fe in the distance. Relief sweeps over me, and my angry fear turns to a mood of wistful longing. For the next mile I think, nostalgically, of home. Europe. The tightly tucked up towns and villages of Bavaria, of Lake Garda and the Dolomites, of Scotland and Wales, of England. Their narrow, winding roads, and twisting curving streets, their well-lit pavements, their dawdling cars, their cyclists and dog walkers, their corner shops and cafes blazing with light.

From *Windswept*, 2021

TIFFANY FRANCIS BAKER

– Remember To . . . –

Remember to wrap up warmly no matter the season. It's surprising how quickly the temperature drops after the sun goes down. A flask of hot chocolate or coffee will also help keep the cold at bay.

If plunging into pitch darkness alone sounds unnerving, start small. Invite a friend and visit your nightwalk location in daylight first to make sure you know your way around. Landscapes change in the dark, so look out for landmarks that will still be visible by starlight.

Take a fully charged smartphone if possible, as you never know when you might need a map or a built-in torch. You can download a stargazing app to identify constellations, or a birdsong app to identify different owl calls.

Nightwalks are the perfect way to get closer to Nature, so to avoid scaring away more elusive species tread softly, whisper quietly and keep artificial lights to a minimum.

From *Resurgence and Ecologist*, 2020

VIRGINIA WOOLF

– In the Darkness the Brain Constructs a Scheme of the World –

In those silences which came too frequently the identity of the figure walking beside me seemed to merge into the night; one strode on alone, conscious of the pressure of the dark all around, conscious too, that by degrees resistance to it grew less and less; that the body carried forward over the ground was something separate from the mind which floated away as though in a swoon. The road even had been left behind, and we had struck – if a word implying definite action can be used of anything as indefinite as our course now became, across the fields of day-time – the trackless ocean of the night. From time to time it was advisable to test the ground beneath the feet in order that its substance might be proved indisputably. Both eyes and ears were fast sealed or, for the pressure on them was of something intangible, had grown numb insensibly, so that the apparition of several lights beneath us had to be realised almost with conscious effort. Could one really see, as in the daytime, or was this some vision within the brain like those stars which a blow scatters before the eye. There they hung, floating without anchorage, in soft depths of darkness in a valley beneath us; for directly that the eye had proved them true the brain woke and constructed a scheme of the world in which to place them. There, too, must be a hill, a town beneath it, the road winding round as we remembered it; a dozen lights can do much to solidify the world. The strangest part of our pilgrimage was over, for something visible had emerged; we had a proof before us. Moreover we found ourselves upon a road, and walked more freely. There were human beings down there too, though they were not as the people of the daytime are. Suddenly a light burnt close at our side, and even as we saw it bearing down upon us a wheel crunched, and a man in a cart was lit up before us; in a second his lights were out and his wheels were dumb; no voice of ours could have reached him. Again, as though scenes were passed swiftly before us and withdrawn, we found ourselves in a farmyard, where a lantern swung an unsteady disc of light over the huddled shapes of cattle, and even discovered parts of our submerged persons. The voice of the farmer bidding us good-night recalled, as though a firm hand had grasped ours, to the shores of the world, but in two strides the immense flood of darkness and silence was over us again. Yet once more lights stood beside us, as though they had approached with silent steps like the lights of ships passing at sea – the lamps we had seen from the hill-top. The village was quiet, but not asleep, as though it lay wide-eyed in tacit conflict with the dark; we could distinguish forms leaning against the house walls, men apparently, who could not sleep with that weight of night pressing against their windows, but must come forth and stretch their arms in it. How puny were the rays of the lamp against the immeasurable waves of darkness swerving around them! A ship at sea is a lonely thing, but far lonelier it seemed was this little village anchored to the desolate earth and exposed every night, alone, to the unfathomed waters of darkness.

And yet, once accustomed to the strange element, there was great peace and beauty in it. It seemed as though only the phantoms and the spirits of substantial things were now abroad; clouds floated where the hills had been, and the houses were sparks of fire. The eye might bathe and refresh itself in the depths of the night, without grating upon any harsh outline of reality; the earth with its infinity of detail was dissolved into ambiguous space. The walls of the house were too narrow, the glare of the lamps too fierce for those thus refreshed and made sensitive; we were as birds lately winged that have been caught and caged.

From the *Guardian*, 1905

FRANZ KAFKA

– The Second –

If we happen to be walking along a street at night, and a man, visible already from afar – because the street inclines gently uphill in front of us, and there's a full moon – comes running towards us, then we will not grab hold of him, even if he's feeble and ragged, even if someone is running after him, yelling, but rather we will let him run on unmolested.

For it is night, and it is not our fault that the street in front of us in the moonlit night is on an incline and, moreover, it is possible that the two men have devised their chase for their own amusement, perhaps they are both in pursuit of a third man, perhaps the first of them is being unjustly pursued, perhaps the second means to kill him and we would become accessory to his murder, perhaps the two of them don't know the first thing about one another and each one is just running home to bed on his own account, perhaps they are two somnambulists, perhaps the first of them is carrying a weapon.

And finally, may we not be tired, and have we not had a lot of wine to drink? We are relieved not to see the second man.

From 'The Men Running Past', 1912,
translated by Michael Hofmann, 2007

– A Third –

The main range, where it appeared in revelations behind us through the clouds, was far higher than mountains ever seem to waking men, and it stood quite sheer as does a precipice in a dream. The forests upon either side of us ran up until they were lost for miles and miles above in the evening storm.

When night fell we still strode onward – one of us never daring to fall far behind the other, and once or twice an hour calling to the other to make sure that the other man was near. But we did not continue this. Because as we went on, under the midnight, each of us became aware of the presence of . . . a third.

From *Hills and the Sea*, 1906

VICTOR HUGO

– Los Demonios? Contrabandistas? –

The old woman lighted a candle-end, and it flashed out from a huge lantern of stamped-tin, tastefully made, hanging before the altar. This feeble light took away nothing from the darkness and added something to the horror. The priest ascended to the altar by a wide step enclosed by a massive stone balustrade.

The old woman was in some obscure corner. The door was left open, and I could see in the distance the country already covered with shadows of the night, the sky growing dark, the bay a vast dry strand; in the foreground a ruin of what had once been a cottage; in the middle distance a ruin of what had been an alcalde's house; in the background the ruin of a convent.

At that instant a noise came to my ears. I listened, not being able to believe it, and listened again. The band of children who had followed me here had seen the church-door open. They came and took their places in the porch, and then sang at the tops of their voices, derisively and with shrieks of laughter, the mass and the vesper service, parodying the priest at the altar and the choir in the chancel.

Need I tell you, my friend, at this moment I felt

in my heart of hearts a pity for these poor children, deprived of religion before they are furnished with civilisation.

And then, from the children, my pity extended to this poor old nave of the Holy Office, obliged silently to endure the insult. What a punishment! What a reaction! Children making sport of what for so long has made men tremble! Oh, if stones had hearts, what wrath must be stirring in the foundations of these walls! And to think it was taking place only a few miles from the valley of Loyola!

While the children were singing, the nave grew darker and darker, and the night filling the church seemed to be the image of the night which was coming over their faith. Melancholy church of Saint-Dominique!

It was dark night when I set off from the church. All the windows and doors in the village were tightly closed. Not a light, not a native. One would think that these sepulchres had been shut up once more, and that these spectres had gone back to sleep.

But at one place I made out a faint light. I continued towards it, and saw in a low chamber an old woman crouching down motionless, with her back against a newly whitewashed wall. Above her head burned a lamp attached to a nail – an ancient lamp, shaped like a sepulchral lamp. It seemed to me that I was looking on Lady Macbeth.

The light of this light allowed me to read over

the door of the house opposite an inscription: POSADA LHABIT.

I was ready to find anything here but not an inn. The moon was rising behind the mountains as I made out from the village. Now it was easy for me to find my way back. Nevertheless, in the state of mind produced by this strange place, I found it difficult to recognise the landscape which had so charmed me a few hours before. This region, so gay in the sunlight, became lugubrious in the moonlight. The solitude of night filled the horizon.

Soon I was approaching Pasages. Here and there travellers began to appear along the road. I had my eyes fastened on the ruin of a castillo which stood out in the moonlight, on the crest of a high mountain, rising from a narrow and wild valley.

What disturbed me was a light beginning to show in the ruin, at the end of the gable. There was something inexplicable and strange about it: first due to the place it was shining from, and secondly because of the way in which it shined. It acted like a revolving light, shining brightly, then disappearing, then flaring up again, and shining out suddenly like a great star. What was that fire, and what did it mean?

As I reached the gorge with the bridge – there came the poor woman whom I found at the entrance of the ropewalk every morning. She gave a slight benefaction, and was crossing the road on the way to her cottage, half-way up the hill. When she saw me she turned round, made the sign of the cross and pointed to the light: 'Los demonios' – 'The demons.'

I went on my way.

A little farther, at the entrance of a steep-paved slope, running down to Pasages, a man, a fisherman, was standing on a block of red marble and, like the old woman, was looking directly at the Light: 'Que es eso?' – 'What is that ?' I asked, as I came upon him.

The man did not take his eyes from the light, and whispered: 'Contrabandistas' – 'Smugglers!'

Later on, returning to my room, my landlady, the excellent Madame Basquetz came to me:

'Monsieur, how late you are! You have not had anything to eat, have you? Where have you been walking?'

'At Leso.'

'Ah! You have been at Leso?'

'Yes, madame.'

She repeated a moment later with a pensive air:

'At Leso?'

'Why, yes,' said I. 'Have you never been there?'

'No, sir.'

'And why not?'

'Because here we never go to Leso.'

'And why don't you ever go there?'

'I . . . I don't know.'

From *Victor Hugo's Letters to his Wife and Others*,
translated by Nathan Haskell Dole, 1895

JOSEPH ADDISON

– Night Heightens the Awfulness of the Place –

Terror everywhere attacks my spirits, and the very silence terrifies me. – Virgil

At a little distance from Sir Roger's House, among the Ruins of an old Abby, there is a long Walk of aged Elms; which are shot up so very high, that when one passes under them, the Rooks and Crows that rest upon the Tops of them seem to be cawing in another Region. I am very much delighted with this Sort of Noise, which I consider as a kind of natural Prayer to that Being who supplies the Wants of his whole Creation, and who, in the beautiful Language of the Psalms feedeth the young Ravens that call upon him. I like this promenade the better, because of an ill Report it lies under of being *haunted* for which Reason (as I have been told in the Family) no living Creature ever walks in it besides the Chaplain. My good Friend the Butler desired me with a very grave Face not to venture myself in it after Sunset, for that one of the Footmen had been almost frighted out of his Wits by a Spirit that appear'd to him in the Shape of a black Horse without an Head; to which he added, that about a Month ago one of the Maids coming home late that way with a Pail of Milk upon her Head, heard such a Rustling among the Bushes that she let the Pail fall. I was taking a Walk in this Place last Night and could not but fancy it one of the most proper Scenes in the World for a Ghost to appear in. The Ruins of the Abby are scattered up and down on every Side, and half covered with Ivy and Elder-Bushes, the Harbours of several solitary Birds which seldom make their Appearance till the Dusk of the Evening. The Place was formerly a Churchyard, and has still several Marks in it of Graves and Burying-Places.

There is such an Eccho among the old Ruins and Vaults, that if you stamp but a little louder than ordinary, you hear the Sound repeated. At the same time the Walk of Elms, with the Croaking of the Ravens which from time to time are heard from the Tops of them, looks exceeding solemn and venerable. These Objects naturally raise Seriousness and Attention; and when Night heightens the Awfulness of the Place, and pours out her supernumerary Horrors upon everything in it, I do not at all wonder that weak Minds fill it with Spectres and Apparitions. Mr Locke, in his Chapter of the Association of Ideas, has very curious Remarks to shew how by the Prejudice of Education one Idea often introduces into the Mind a whole Set that bear no Resemblance to one another in the Nature of things. Among several Examples of this Kind, he produces the following Instance:

> The Ideas of Goblins and Sprights have really no more to do with Darkness than Light: Yet let but a foolish Maid inculcate these often on the Mind of a Child, and raise them there together, possibly he shall never be able to separate them again so long as he lives; but Darkness shall ever afterwards bring with it those frightful Ideas, and they shall be so joined, that he can no more bear the one than the other.

As I was walking in this Solitude, where the Dark of the Evening conspired with so many other Occasions of Terror, I observed a Cow grazing not far from me, which an Imagination that is apt to startle might easily have construed into a black Horse without an Head: And I dare say the poor Footman who was roaming in the dark here lost his Wits upon some such an Occasion.

From the *Spectator*, July 6, 1711

MARY KINGSLEY

– Witches Eating Crabs –

I think I may say that every dangerous place here is regarded as the residence of a god – rocks, and whirlpools in the rivers – and swamps where 'no man is fit to wander' and, naturally, the surf. Along the Gold Coast, every place where you walk through the surf fairly swarms with gods.

There is one thing about this that I do not understand – and that is why witches always walk stark naked along the beach at night, and eat sea crabs the while. That such is a confirmed habit of theirs is certain; and they tell me that while doing this the witches emit a bright light, and also that there is a certain medicine, which, if you have with you, you can throw over the witch, and he, or she, will remain blazing until morning time, running to and fro, crying out wildly, in front of the white, breaking, thundering surf wall, and when the dawn comes the fire burns the witch right up, leaving only a grey ash – and palaver sets in this world and the next for that witch.

A highly-esteemed minister told me when I was at Cape Coast last, that a fortnight before, he had been away in the Apollonia district on mission work. One evening he and a friend were walking along the beach and the night was dark, so that you could see only the surf. It is never too dark to see that. It seems to have light in itself. They saw a flame coming towards them, and after a moment's doubt they knew it was a witch, and feeling frightened, hid themselves among the bushes that edge the sandy shore. As they watched, it came straight on and passed them, and they saw it disappear into the distance. My informant laughed at himself, and very wisely said, 'One has not got to believe these things here, that one has in Apollonia.'

From *Travels in West Africa*, 1897

RACHEL CARSON

– Ghost Crab –

Once, exploring the night beach, I surprised a small ghost crab in the searching beam of my torch. He was lying in a pit he had dug just above the surf, as though watching the sea and waiting. The blackness of the night possessed water, air, and beach. It was the darkness of an older world, before Man. There was no sound but the all-enveloping primeval sounds of wind blowing over water and sand, and of waves crashing on the beach. There was no other visible life – just one small crab near the sea. I have seen hundreds of ghost crabs in other settings, but suddenly I was filled with the odd sensation that for the first time I knew the creature in its own world – that I understood as never before the essence of its being. In that moment time was suspended; the world to which I belonged did not exist and I might have been an onlooker from outer space. The little crab alone with the sea became a symbol that stood for life itself – for the delicate, destructible, yet incredibly vital force that somehow holds its place amid the harsh realities of the inorganic world.

From *The Edge of the Sea*, 1955

AMELIA B. EDWARDS

– Gleaming Teeth –

We have been tracing all the preparations for a great religious ceremony. We have seen the king enter the temple; undergo the symbolical purification; receive the twofold crown; and say his prayers to each divinity in turn. We have followed him into the laboratories, the oratories, and the holy of holies. All that he has yet done, however, is preliminary. The procession is yet to come, and here we have it. Here, sculptured on the walls of this dark staircase, the crowning ceremony of worship is brought before our eyes in all its details. Here, one by one, we have the standard-bearers, the hierophants with the offerings, the priests, the whole long, wonderful procession, with the king marching at its head. Fresh and uninjured, as if they had just left the hand of the sculptor, these figures – each in his habit as he lived, each with his foot upon the step – mount with us as we mount, and walk beside us all the way. Their attitudes are so natural, their forms so roundly cut, that one could almost fancy them in motion as the lights flicker by. Surely there must be one weird night in the year when they step out from their places and take up the next verse of their chanted hymn, and, to the sound of instruments long mute and songs long silent, pace the moonlit roof in ghostly order!

At length we emerge upon that vast terrace. The roofing-stones are gigantic. Striding to and fro over some of the biggest, we find several that measure seven paces in length by four in breadth. In the distant corner, like a little stone lodge in a vast courtyard, stands a small temple supported on columns; while at the eastern end, forming a second and loftier stage, rises the roof of the portico.

Meanwhile, the mountains are clothed in an atmosphere of darkness; mysterious shadows are creeping over the plain, and the mounds of the ancient city lie at our feet, confused and tumbled, like the waves of a black sea. How high it is here. How lonely. How silent. Hark that thin, plaintive cry! It is the wail of a night-wandering jackal. See how dark it is, in the direction of the river. Quick, quick! We have lingered too long. We must be gone at once; for we are already benighted.

We ought to have gone down by way of the opposite staircase (which is lined with sculptures of the descending procession) and out through the temple; but there is no time to do anything but scramble down by a breach in the wall at a point where the mounds lie heaped against the south side of the building. Then before we reach the bottom we can hardly see where to tread. The huge side wall of the portico seems to tower above us to the very heavens.

We catch a glimpse of two colossal figures, one lion-headed and the other headless, sitting outside with backs to the temple. Then, making with all speed for the open plain, we clamber over scattered blocks and among shapeless mounds. Night overtakes us. The mountains disappear; the temple is blotted out; and we have only the faint starlight to guide us. We stumble on, keeping all close together; firing a gun every now and then, in the hope of being heard by those in the boats; and as thoroughly lost as the babes in the wood.

At last, as some are beginning to knock up, and all to despair, Talhamy fires his last cartridge. An answering shot replies nearby; a wandering light appears in the distance; and then a whole bevy of dancing lanterns and friendly faces come shining out from among a plantation of sugarcanes to welcome and guide us home. Dear, sturdy, faithful little Hassan, honest Khalifeh, laughing Salame, gentle Mehemet Ali, and Musa – they were all there. What a shaking of hands there was. What a gleaming of teeth. What a shower of mutually unintelligible congratulations! For my own part, I must say that I had never so rejoiced at a meeting-up in all my life.

From *A Thousand Miles Up the Nile*, 1877

JOHN HILLABY

– Headless –

Several times that evening I thought I heard the sound of voices among the trees and once the bark of a dog. Perhaps a bird or a porcupine, but so dog-like in that quiet broken only by the lapping of the lake . . .

On the way back to the comforting firelight I stopped short at the sight of what appeared to be a hunched-up figure. The headless Indian! Now let me admit at once this was a fantasy provoked by something I had read years ago. But in the gathering dusk, the mossy stump of that pine bore such an uncanny resemblance to what I recalled vividly that I walked round it twice, the better to calm my disordered imagination.

The headless Indian appears in *Primitive Scenes and Festivals* by Sacheverell Sitwell . . . He describes how, over a hundred years ago, two explorers, Lord Milton and Dr D. B. Cheadle of the Royal Geographical Society, were lost for days in pine forest on a long trek from the Atlantic to the Pacific. The story is well authenticated by the diaries kept and subsequently published by the two men in 1865.

They were desperately hungry. Their companion, an Assiniboine, returned that night and flung down an animal, a hare or a marten, saying drily, '*J'ai trouvé rien que cela et un homme – un mort.*'

He directed them to the dead body which was only a few hundred yards from the camp and, after a long search they found that ominous spectacle at the foot of a pine.

The corpse was in a sitting position with the legs crossed and the arms clasped over the knees, bending forward over the miserable ashes of a fire of small sticks. The figure was headless, and the cervical vertebrae protruded dry and bare; the skin was brown and shrivelled, stretched like parchment over the bony framework . . . The clothes consisted of a woollen shirt and leggings with a tattered blanket still hung round the shrunken form . . .

A heap of broken bones at the skeleton's side – the fragments of a horse's head – told the story of his fate. They were chipped into the smallest pieces, showing that the unfortunate man had died of starvation, and probably existed as far as possible by sucking every particle out of the broken fragments. But where was the head?

They searched diligently, everywhere, but could find no trace of it. As they put it, had it fallen off they should have found it lying nearby, for an animal that dared abstract a portion would have returned to attack the body . . . They could not solve the problem and left the body undisturbed, taking only his little axe for their necessities . . . Lord Milton says they walked back to camp 'silent and full of thought'. And so did I.

From *Journey Through Love*, 1977

LIEUTENANT CHARLES I. HALT

– Unexplained at Approximately 0300 –

Early in the morning of 27 Dec 80 (approximately 0300), two USAF security police patrolmen saw unusual lights outside the back gate at RAF Woodbridge. Thinking an aircraft might have crashed or been forced down, they called for permission to go outside the gate to investigate. The on-duty flight chief responded and allowed three patrolmen to proceed on foot. The individuals reported seeing a strange glowing object in the forest. The object was described as being metallic in appearance and triangular in shape, approximately two to three meters across the base and approximately two meters high. It illuminated the entire forest with a white light. The object itself had a pulsating red light on top and a bank of blue lights underneath. The object was hovering or on legs. As the patrolmen approached the object, it manoeuvred through the trees and disappeared. At this time the animals on a nearby farm went in to a frenzy. The object was briefly sighted approximately an hour later near the back gate.

From 'Memorandum from the Deputy Base Commander', 1981

W. H. HUDSON

– A Little Before 3.45 a.m. –

A cock began to crow. It was a fine still night, without a cloud in the pale, dusky blue sky, thinly sprinkled with stars, and the crescent moon coming up above the horizon. After the cock, a tawny owl began to hoot, and the long tremulous mellow sound followed me for some distance from the village; and then there was perfect silence, broken occasionally by the tinkling bells of a little company of cyclists speeding past towards 'The Stones'. I was in no hurry: I only wished I had started sooner to enjoy Salisbury Plain at its best time, when all the things which offend the lover of nature are invisible and non-existent. Later, when the first light began to appear in the east before two o'clock, it was no false dawn, but grew brighter and spread further, until touches of colour, very delicate, rose and purple, began to show –

The miracle of diuturnity Whose instancy unbeds the lark,
that all the days of my life on which I had not witnessed it were
wasted days!

O that unbedding of the lark! The world that was so still now had a sound; not a single song and not in one place, but a sound composed of a thousand individual sounds, rising out of the dark earth at a distance on my right hand and up into the dusky sky, spreading far and wide – a sound as of multitudinous twanging, girding, and clashing instruments, mingled with shrill piercing voices that were not like the voices of earthly beings. They were not human nor angelic, but passionless, and it was as if the whole visible world, the dim grassy plain and the vast pale sky sprinkled with paling stars, and moonlit, had found a voice to express the mystery and glory of this time.

It was eight minutes past two o'clock when this 'unbedding of the lark' began, and the heavenly music lasted about fourteen minutes, then died down to silence, to recommence about half an hour later. At first I wondered why the sound was at a distance from the road on my right hand and not on my left hand as well. Then I remembered what I had seen on that side, how the 'boys' at play on Sundays and in fact every day hunt the birds and pull their nests out, and I could only conclude that the lark has been pretty well wiped out from all that part of the plain over which the soldiers range.

At Stonehenge I found a good number of watchers, about a couple of hundred, already assembled, and more coming in continually, and a mile or so of the road to Amesbury had at times the appearance of a ribbon of fire from the lamps of this continuous stream of coming cyclists. Altogether five to six hundred persons gathered at 'The Stones', mostly young men on bicycles, who came from all the Wiltshire towns within easy distance. I had a few good minutes at the ancient temple when the sight of the rude upright stones looking black against the moonlit and star-sprinkled sky produced an expected feeling in me: but the mood could not last; the crowd was too big and noisy, and the noises they made too suggestive of a Bank Holiday crowd at the Crystal Palace.

At three o'clock a ribbon of slate-grey cloud appeared above the eastern horizon, and broadened by degrees. At a quarter to four the crowd, sang and shouted; and by and by, just outside the barbed-wire enclosure a rabbit was unearthed, and about three hundred young men with shrieks of excitement set about its capture. It was a lively scene, a general scrimmage, in which everyone was trying to capture an elusive football with ears and legs to it, which went darting and spinning about hither and thither among the multitudinous legs, until earth compassionately opened and swallowed poor distracted bunny up. It was but little better inside the enclosure, where the big fallen stones behind the altar-stone, in the middle, were taken possession of by a crowd who sat and stood packed together like guillemots on a rock. These too wanted to have a little fun, and began to be very obstreperous. By and by they found out an amusement very much to their taste. Motor-cars were now arriving every minute, bringing important-looking persons who had timed their journeys so as to come upon the scene a little before 3.45; and whenever one of these gentlemen appeared within the circle of stones, especially if he was big physically and grotesque-looking in his motorist getup, he was greeted with a tremendous shout. In most cases he would start back and stand still, astonished at such an outburst, and then, concluding that the only way to save his dignity was to face the music, he would step hurriedly across the green space to hide himself behind the crowd. All this proved entertaining, and I was glad to laugh with the crowd, thinking that after all we were taking a mild revenge on our hated enemies – the tyrants of the roads.

From *Afoot in England*, 1909

– The Night Had Gone –

Just before dawn, I came to a cleft high in the hills, so that I could only see a little copse of oak and hazel, and in the dying moonlight a thousand white islands of cloud and mountain.

The night had gone, and the day had not come; and the little copse had the serious, brooding air which all things have at that hour, and especially when the land is tender with the first hope of spring and in that reverie:

Cette reverie que ne pense a rien.

For what I saw seemed but the fragments of something which night had built for its own delight, and as they became clearer and clearer they had more and more the appearance of being unbuilt and dissolved. But, gradually, the birds were let out and they sang. Their songs, on the wintry hill, which I had last visited in summer, broke upon the silence as in summer they never do, like the opening of the door of a room that is empty but has once been gay with fire and books and men; and sweet though the blackbird was, and shrill the missel-thrush, their songs were awful, and said that 'a large part of the earth is still in the urn unto us'. The grass, which had truly been of no colour, though my urgent memory persuaded me that it was green, began to awake to colour, and, while in the shadow of the copse the dusk was impenetrable, the light reached a knoll where there was dead bracken still. 'Colour,' said Novalis, ' is an effort of matter to become light,' and for one moment the grass upon that knoll ceased to strive and was light. A plover that wheeled close by disappeared and was but a glow.

I went on, and on a lower slope the ploughman was beginning to plough in the shadow. Grim and worthless looked the work, until I looked round and saw the dawn that was being prepared. But I watched too carefully, for I saw it all. Ever, as it grew, statelier and richer, I said to myself, that in a little while it would be perfected: yet still I watched and I began to think of those who saw it, as I had seen it before, from windows of towns, as they rose for work, or as they douted the candles and put away cards or books, and paused for perhaps a minute, and gazed as they never gazed at human beauty, because, though they revered it, they feared it also, and though they feared it they were fascinated. I thought of those that leapt up at it; those that mourned because they had seen it pass so often before into a common day; those that, on inhospitable roads, saw it and neglected it, or cursed it after a night in which they had drunk their last poor earnings altogether. If it would but last . . . I had been looking at it and had not seen it, and when I dropped these thoughts I knew that it was gone, the slowly prepared and solemn dawn which made the splendid spring of that year. Then I took a path which led out of sight of the white crested mountain and went down among larches and oaks.

From *Beautiful Wales*, 1905

FLORENCE FENWICK MILLER

– Before Daylight –

In October, 1847, Harriet reached 'The Knoll' again, and settled into her permanent course of home life. The same habits were continued, with only the interruptions of occasional visits to other parts of the country, day by day, for many years.

She rose very early: not infrequently, in the winter, before daylight; and immediately set out for a good, long walk. Sometimes, I am told, she would appear at a farmhouse, four miles off, before the cows were milked. The old post-mistress recollects how, when she was making up her early letter-bags, in the dark of the morning mists, Miss Martineau would come down with her large bundle of correspondence, and never failed to have a pleasant nod and smile, or a few kindly inquiries, for her humble friend.

Writes Miss Martineau to Mr Atkinson, in November, 1847, 'I always go out before it is light, and in the fine mornings I go up the hill behind the church on the Kirkstone road where I reach a great height, and see from halfway along to Rydal. When the little shred of moon that is left and the morning star hang over Wansfell, among the amber clouds of the approaching sunrise, it is delicious. On the positively rainy times, my walk is to Pelter Bridge and back. Sometimes it is round the south end of the valley. These dawn walks (I later sit down to my breakfast at half-past seven) are good, among other things, in preparing me in mind for my work.'

*

Returning home, she breakfasted at half-past seven; filled her lamp ready for the night, and arranged all household matters; and by half-past eight she was at her desk, where she worked undisturbed till two, the early dinnertime. These business hours were sacred to her.

From *Harriet Martineau*, 1884

More Dawns

'Tired of sleeping on a grass pillow, I walked down to the seashore before the break of day:

Early dawn,
Young white fish,
Shining in ephemeral white,
Hardly an inch long.'
– Matsuo Basho

'Black care was sitting on my knapsack; the thoughts would not flow evenly in my mind; sometimes the stream ceased and left me for a second like a dead man. I felt sure I must be going to be ill; and at the same time, I was well aware that a night in the open air and the arrival of the holy and healthy dawn would put me alright again with the world – and also with myself.' – Robert Louis Stevenson

'I awoke at dawn to the didididididi call of the Grey Drongo (probably); the chatterings and mutterings and babblings of unseen babblers (perhaps); the flutings and whistlings and cat-calls of hidden pittas or bulbuls or cuckoo-shrikes or laughing shrushes (maybe); and the distant hoot of a gibbon (certainly).'
– Redmond O'Hanlon

‘The following morning the birds started singing to salute the first light of dawn, and I started off again.’
– Vincent van Gogh

‘Twelve thousand years since the Caveman stood at the mouth of his cavern and gazed out at the night and the stars. He looked again, and saw the sun rise beyond the sea. He closed his eyes. He was face to face with the earth, the night, the sun . . . and face to face with himself.’ – Richard Jefferies

‘Eastward a veil of luminous gauze glowed ever brighter, revealing a rim of gold, then of a sudden blazed fiery flames and out of them leapt the new day. My veins tingled. I thrilled with the knowledge that I, too, shared in the expectancy, the opportunity, the adventure of a new day. Perhaps these things are the most essential to our well-being.’
– Nancy Price

‘What a sunrise behind me. The clouds had split open a crack; and yes, a sun, like the one that rises bloodied on the day of Battle.’ – Werner Herzog

– Acknowledgements –

As ever with the business of anthologising, a number of people have helped illumine the way ahead, this time through the hours 'twixt dusk and dawn. My thanks go to the ever brilliant Notting Hill Editions – to Rosalind Porter, Kim Kremer, Emma O'Bryen, Vera Sugar, Matthew Burne and Deborah Pike. Thanks also to Robin Dennis, Annabel Abbs, Rory Ross, Angela Minshull, Rex and Buddy, Maisie and Doris. And to Harland Miller, an indigo enthusiast, who produced the perfect cover for the book you are holding, called 'Sleepwalkers of the World Rule Ok'.

Review Books as *Paris Vagabond* by Jean-Paul Clébert, translated by Donald Nicholson-Smith. Translation copyright © 2016 by Donald Nicholson-Smith. Used by permission of New York Review Books.

Excerpt from *The Night Country* by Loren Eiseley. Copyright © 1947 by Loren Eiseley. Used by permission of Bison Books, an imprint of University of Nebraska Press.

Extract from 'Pregnant Pause' by Tiffany Francis-Baker. Originally published in *Resurgence & Ecologist*. 2020. Copyright © 2020 by Tiffany-Francis-Baker. Used by permission of the author.

Extract from *Journey through Love* by John Hillaby. Copyright © 1976 by John Hillaby.

Extract from *Metamorphosis* by Franz Kafka, translated by Michael Hoffman, published by Penguin Classics. Translation copyright © Michael Hofmann, 2007. Reprinted by permission of Penguin Books Limited.

Extract from 'Lost' by Joanna Kavenna, originally commissioned for *Where My Feet Fall: Going for a Walk in Twenty Stories* (William Collins). Copyright © 2022 by Joanna Kavenna. Used by permission of the author.

Extract from *Rosehill: Portraits from a Midlands City & More from Rosehill* by Carol Lake. Copyright © 1989, 2024 by Carol Lake. Used by permission of Five Leaves Publications.

Extract from *Nothing to Declare: Memoirs of a Woman Traveling Alone* by Mary Morris. Copyright © 1988 by Mary Morris. Used by permission of HarperCollins Publishers.

Extract from 'Nightwalks' by Kate Pullinger from BBC Radio

3's *The Essay*. Copyright © 2007 by Kate Pullinger. Used by permission of the author.

Extract from 'Letter to Clara Rilke' from *Letters of Rainer Maria Rilke: 1892–1910*, translated by Jane Bannard Greene and M. D. Herter Norton. Copyright © 1945 by W. W. Norton & Company, Inc., renewed © 1972 by M. D. Herter Norton. Used by permission of W. W. Norton & Company, Inc.

Extract from *A Woman in the Polar Night* by Christiane Ritter, translated by Jane Degras. First published in 1938 as *Eine Frau erlebt die Polarnacht.* First published in English in 1954 by George Allen & Unwin Ltd, London. English translation copyright © 1954 by Jane Degras. Used by permission of Pushkin Press.

Extract from *The Rings of Saturn* by W. G. Sebald published by Harvill Press. Copyright © Vito von Eichborn Verlag, Frankfurt am Main, 1995, used by permission of The Wylie Agency (UK). English translation copyright © Michael Hulse, 1998. Reprinted by permission of The Random House Group Limited.

Extract from *Lot's Wife, and Some Reflections on Walking at Night* by Nicholas Shakespeare, originally commissioned for *Where My Feet Fall: Going for a Walk in Twenty Stories* (William Collins). Copyright © 2022 by Nicholas Shakespeare. Used by permission of the author.

'"Well, good night. I'm going to go and listen to the nightingales." And I walked off.'

– George Sand